PUBLICATIONS OF
THE INSTITUTE OF HIGHER EDUCATION

LIBERAL EDUCATION AND JOURNALISM
Paul L. Dressel

LIBERAL EDUCATION AND ENGINEERING
Edwin J. Holstein and Earl J. McGrath

LIBERAL EDUCATION AND PHARMACY
James Newcomer, Kevin P. Bunnell, and Earl J. McGrath

LIBERAL EDUCATION AND MUSIC
Willis J. Wager and Earl J. McGrath

LIBERAL EDUCATION AND BUSINESS
William M. Kephart, James E. McNulty, and Earl J. McGrath

LIBERAL EDUCATION AND HOME ECONOMICS
Jeanette A. Lee and Paul L. Dressel

THE ACADEMIC DEANSHIP
John Wesley Gould

COOPERATIVE LONG-RANGE PLANNING IN LIBERAL ARTS COLLEGES
Earl J. McGrath

THE PREDOMINANTLY NEGRO COLLEGES AND UNIVERSITIES IN TRANSITION
Earl J. McGrath

LIBERAL EDUCATION IN THE SERVICE ACADEMIES
William E. Simons

LIBERAL EDUCATION AND SOCIAL WORK
Gordon J. Aldridge and Earl J. McGrath

SELECTED ISSUES IN HIGHER EDUCATION
AN ANNOTATED BIBLIOGRAPHY
L. Richard Meeth

ARTS COLLEGE AND THE EMERGENT CASTE SYSTEM
Earl J. McGrath

THE LIBERAL ARTS COLLEGE'S RESPONSIBILITY FOR THE INDIVIDUAL STUDENT
Earl J. McGrath

SELECTED ISSUES IN COLLEGE ADMINISTRATION
Earl J. McGrath

GENERAL EDUCATION IN HIGHER EDUCATION
Aston R. Williams

THE CHANGING MISSION OF HOME ECONOMICS
Earl J. McGrath and *Jack T. Johnson*

NEW PROSPECTS FOR THE SMALL LIBERAL ARTS COLLEGE
Sidney S. Letter

INNOVATION IN LIBERAL ARTS COLLEGES
Michael Brick and *Earl J. McGrath*

INNOVATION IN
LIBERAL ARTS COLLEGES

MICHAEL BRICK

Associate Director, Institute of Higher Education

EARL J. McGRATH

Director, Institute of Higher Education

PUBLISHED FOR THE

INSTITUTE OF HIGHER EDUCATION

BY

TEACHERS COLLEGE PRESS

TEACHERS COLLEGE, COLUMBIA UNIVERSITY

To BARRETT LEE BRICK
MY GREATEST INNOVATION

—M.B.

CONTENTS

Chapter 1

INNOVATIONS AND THE LIBERAL ARTS COLLEGE

ONE FACT ABOUT THE PRESENT SITUATION OF AMERICAN COLLEGES AND universities which probably overshadows all others is the widespread feeling that the American system of higher education is under stress. Throughout the United States colleges and universities are engaged in extensive reappraisal of their programs. As these reappraisals are going on, the colleges find themselves faced with the increasing pressure of greater numbers of students seeking admission and the problem of obtaining enough teachers to provide the kinds of instruction these students want and need.

One concern raised by the study of American higher education is the fate of the liberal arts college. In 1963, Jacques Barzun, then dean of faculties and provost of Columbia University, said bluntly that he considered the liberal arts college tradition dead or dying—much to his regret. This dire warning note was sounded at a time when never before in our national life had the demand for general and broad knowledge, combined with the capacity for independent intellectual activity, been so acute. Contrary to the prophets of doom, however, most liberal arts colleges are neither dead nor dying. It is an indisputable fact that today most of these institutions can get as many students as their faculties and buildings can accommodate.

Those who express doubt about their future may have more reason for concern on qualitative rather than on quantitative grounds. A successful liberal arts college has a faculty dedicated to the profession of teaching and working with young people. The faculty must recognize that it is their job

1

to create the kind of environment in which learning can take place. Five hundred years ago, before Gutenberg, knowledge was preserved and transmitted by being laboriously memorized, or equally laboriously transcribed by hand into books. Today most college classes are conducted as though Gutenberg had never existed. The teacher lectures and the students occupy themselves with tediously copying his words into their notes. It may be that this is the most efficient of all possible processes for learning. But the evidence indicates overwhelmingly that it is a hopelessly inefficient— indeed a nearly totally ineffective—process. The faculty needs to design a total environment on campus to achieve effective learning, keeping in mind that learning depends only on what the student does, and not (except indirectly) on what the teacher does; learning depends on what the student does outside the classroom as well as within; there are ascertainable and definable differences between rote and meaningful learning.

It was a desire on the part of the Carnegie Foundation for the Advancement of Teaching to try to ascertain some of the trends and thrusts on liberal arts college campuses of the country in regard to innovative practices that led to the study reported here. The purpose of the study was to develop a picture of novel and creative practices that were introduced in the liberal arts colleges in the United States in recent years. The authors of the present report were to describe these practices that were innovative and in the process try to identify innovative institutions. We hypothesized that most knowledge of what was taking place in liberal arts education was based on a select few institutions and there possibly might be other institutions engaged in innovative educational practices that were little known to the educational world. We hoped to identify and describe such institutions.

In choosing the population for the study we decided that we could not use random sampling. We therefore polled all four-year institutions in the United States which offered a program of liberal arts. In order to determine our sample, we used the *Education Directory,* Part 3, *Higher Education,* published by the U.S. Department of Health, Education, and Welfare, 1965–1966. We sent our questionnaire (included as Appendix A of this study) to those institutions that were classified as four-year colleges and were designated as having a liberal arts program.[1]

---

[1] Institutions are classified in the Directory as follows: I. 2 but less than 4 years of work beyond the 12th grade; II. Only the bachelor's and/or first professional degree; III. Master's and/or second professional degree; IV. Doctor of philosophy and equivalent degrees; and V. Other. The designations of institutions by type of program are as follows: *a.* Terminal-occupational (below bachelor's degree); *b.* Liberal arts and general; *c.* Liberal arts and general, and terminal-occupational; *d.* Primarily teacher preparatory; *e.* Liberal arts and general, and teacher

In using this method we included in our population very diverse institutions. We included, of course, liberal arts colleges such as Reed, Antioch, Earlham; we included colleges of arts and science of large universities such as Berkeley, Michigan, Arkansas, Florida; we also included many small church-related institutions which were listed by the directory as offering liberal arts programs, such as Dunbarton College of Holy Cross, Sacred Heart University, and St. Joseph College. We found the approach satisfactory for it allowed us complete coverage; it allowed us to make comparisons between institutions; and it also allowed us to check our hypothesis that innovation was not limited to the larger, prestigious colleges.

For the purpose of the present study, we defined an innovation as an idea, thing, or process which is new to higher education, the "newness" often stemming from a rearrangement of an accepted procedure in such a way that it reaps novel benefits. Accordingly, we hold that an innovation in higher education frequently enables a college or university to increase the efficiency of some aspect of operation.

In setting forth "newness" as a requisite feature of innovation, we note that this characteristic is mentioned by various authorities. For example, *Webster's New World Dictionary* defines innovation as ". . . something newly introduced; new method, custom, device, etc.; change in the way of doing things."[2] Furthermore, H. G. Barnett, a student of the sociology of innovation, writes, "an innovation is here defined as any thought, behavior, or thing that is new because it is qualitatively different from existing forms . . . innovation and novelty are hereafter used synonymously."[3] Finally, Matthew B. Miles of Teachers College, Columbia University, states that "the element of novelty, implying recombination of parts or a qualitative difference from existing forms, seems quite essential . . . [to the definition of innovation]."[4]

Although we consider newness or novelty to be a vital counterpart of innovation, we think that this quality may arise from the alteration of an

---

preparatory; *f.* Liberal arts and general, teacher preparatory, and terminal-occupational; *g.* Professional only; *h.* Professional and teacher preparatory; *i.* Professional and terminal-occupational; *j.* Liberal arts and general with 1 or 2 professional schools; and *k.* Liberal arts and general with 3 or more professional schools. For the study we sent a questionnaire to all institutions designated as II, III, and IV, and *b, c, e, f, j,* or *k.*

[2] *Webster's New World Dictionary,* College Edition, 1964.

[3] Homer G. Barnett, *Innovation: The Basis of Cultural Change* (New York: McGraw-Hill Book Company, 1953), p. 7.

[4] Matthew B. Miles, editor, *Innovation in Education* (New York: Teachers College Press, Teachers College, Columbia University, 1964), p. 14.

TABLE 1   RESPONDENT COLLEGES, BY STATE

State	Number of Colleges	Number of Colleges Responding	Number of Usable Responses
Alabama	22	19	19
Alaska	2	2	2
Arizona	4	4	4
Arkansas	17	15	15
California	72	54	51
Colorado	12	10	10
Connecticut	19	15	15
Delaware	2	2	2
District of Columbia	11	7	6
Florida	17	14	14
Georgia	26	20	19
Guam	1	1	1
Hawaii	3	2	1
Idaho	4	3	3
Illinois	53	41	41
Indiana	31	23	23
Iowa	28	24	24
Kansas	26	21	19
Kentucky	23	17	17
Louisiana	19	12	11
Maine	9	9	8
Maryland	24	19	18
Massachusetts	47	33	31
Michigan	32	26	25
Minnesota	24	19	19

existing form or the employment of that form in a different mode, rather than arising exclusively from a totally new creation. To support this point of view, Stanley J. Heywood asserts

. . . an innovation is not necessarily "new" in the sense that it has not been tried before. The basic innovation may be a return to a method or procedure that is "old" in the sense that it has been used before. Usually, however, there are new components.[5]

The denotation of some educational procedure or entity as an innovation, we believe, is contingent on individual or group perceptions within a given social context. Therefore, it follows that when some time-hon-

[5] Stanley J. Heywood, "Toward a Sound Theory of Innovation," *Elementary School Journal,* 66:107–114, December 1965, p. 108.

TABLE 1   RESPONDENT COLLEGES, BY STATE *(Continued)*

State	Number of Colleges	Number of Colleges Responding	Number of Usable Responses
Mississippi	16	10	10
Missouri	34	29	26
Montana	7	5	4
Nebraska	15	13	12
Nevada	1	0	0
New Hampshire	11	8	7
New Jersey	18	13	13
New Mexico	8	6	6
New York	96	73	65
North Carolina	40	29	29
North Dakota	9	6	6
Ohio	52	42	40
Oklahoma	19	14	13
Oregon	19	14	13
Pennsylvania	85	68	64
Puerto Rico	5	2	2
Rhode Island	8	4	3
South Carolina	23	13	11
South Dakota	12	10	10
Tennessee	37	29	27
Texas	54	37	36
Utah	6	5	4
Vermont	10	8	7
Virginia	30	23	23
Washington	15	12	11
West Virginia	16	14	14
Wisconsin	34	28	27
Wyoming	1	1	1
TOTAL	1,209	928	882

ored educational practice is transposed from its prior context to a new one, the practice may be justifiably termed an innovation by the members of the new social context, should these individuals perceive the practice as a new one. Our opinion concerning the role of human perception in the definition of innovation is consistent with the writings of E. M. Rogers, who states:

An innovation is an idea perceived as new by the individual. It really matters little, as far as human behavior is concerned, whether or not an idea is "objectively" new as measured by the amount of time elapsed since its first use or discovery. It is the newness of the idea to the individual that determines his reaction to it.[6]

In order to collect data on innovative practices, we decided to send out a screening questionnaire which would allow administrators to indicate whether or not their institutions had the practice; when the practice was introduced—the key dates being prior to 1961 and 1961 and after; if they did not have the practice, did they plan to introduce it; and in some instances, was the practice used on a college-wide basis, a departmental basis, or by an individual faculty member.[7] In addition, open-ended questions allowed administrators to:

1.   Indicate whether they felt their college was innovative and also to identify innovative faculty members on the campus.

2.   Describe the practices they considered to be most imaginative, novel, or vital of those introduced on the campus since 1961.

The questionnaire was sent to 1,209 colleges of which 928 colleges or 76.8 per cent responded. (See Table 1.) Of the responses, 882 were usable, which represents 73.0 per cent of the total number of colleges surveyed. A large majority of the institutions not responding were small, church-related institutions that had very small student enrollments.

The responses of the 882 institutions were tabulated and follow-up letters were sent to the presidents of the colleges asking for detailed descriptions of the practices they had indicated existed on their campus. In every instance, a response ranging from 70 to 90 per cent was received for every item on the questionnaire.

[6] Everett M. Rogers, *Diffusion of Innovations* (New York: The Free Press, 1962), p. 13.
[7] See Appendix A.

Chapter 2

NEW APPROACHES TO THE CURRICULUM

As INSTITUTIONS CONTINUE TO EXPAND AND ADJUST THEIR PURPOSES TO meet new demands, the curriculum obviously becomes a major focus of attention. Many of today's college students are thoroughly bored with their course work. At a time when they are asking the big questions about themselves and the world, they find few, if any, answers in their education. What they do find has little relevance to what they are experiencing. These jolting truths have been perceived on many college campuses throughout the country and various attempts at curricula reform have been undertaken.

Curricular developments in liberal arts colleges have attempted to respond to a number of issues that are as old as "the arguments of Socrates against the Sophists and as new as the difference between Clark Kerr's conception of the multi-versity and Robert M. Hutchins' continued emphasis upon the liberal arts."[1] These issues are:

1. The question of "cash versus culture."[2] Should the college stress classical literature, moral philosophy, and natural philosophy or should it stress the application of knowledge to specific tasks?

2. The matter of the general vs. the specific. Should students be introduced to broad overviews of domains of knowledge, or should they be required to concentrate effort in a limited field? The issue involves the

[1] Lewis B. Mayhew, *The Collegiate Curriculum: An Approach to Analysis* (Atlanta, Georgia: Southern Regional Education Board, no date), p. 1.
[2] R. Freeman Butts, *The College Charts Its Course* (New York: McGraw-Hill Book Company, 1939).

struggle between the departmental emphasis on disciplinary courses and the pleas of theorists for broad interdisciplinary courses.

3.   Should the courses and programs be student- or subject-oriented? Related is the question as to whether the curriculum, or significant parts of it, should be discipline- or problem-oriented.

If one examines recent attempts at curricula construction, one finds a struggle to accommodate all these issues. Two major changes in Baker University's academic program introduced in the fall of 1968 illustrate curricular developments in liberal arts colleges across the country. One change is a new academic calendar which makes room for five weeks of study each year on the tutorial system. Dubbed the 4–1–4 (for the number of study units each term), it includes two sixteen-week semesters separated by an interterm in which each student will do intensive work on a limited topic, under close supervision of one professor.[3]

The more radical change at this Methodist liberal arts school is a six-semester core curriculum—one course each semester of the freshman, sophomore, and junior years—which ignores the traditional categories of knowledge. It pulls together information and ideas from many disciplines to focus on the theme, Man's Search for Meaning. William C. Young, architect of the new curriculum, said he knows of no other college which has used a thematic approach for an entire sequence of core courses.

Under the new Baker plan, every semester six or seven professors will prepare a lecture for each of the three classes. Twice a week, for an hour, they address the whole class. This is followed immediately by an hour of discussion in groups of no more than fourteen students, each led by a faculty member. While the lecturers will be experts on their topics, the discussion leaders will be out of their fields.

The six-semester core curriculum starts with Man Discovers Himself to help students learn first of all about themselves. Religion, mythology, anthropology, medicine, and science are some of the fields tapped in lectures, readings, and films as students probe man's nature. Next, in the unit Man Discovers the Universe, they study science as a predictive instrument and problems of applying scientific knowledge. The third unit, at the start of the sophomore year, is Man's Modern Predicament—his search for meaning and self-understanding in a world where he feels alienation and where there is an apparent crisis of values. Next, in Man Examines His Society, students move through political systems to such topics as the population explosion, the technological revolution, crime, race and racism, mass education, and the age of overkill. Finally, be-

---

[3] See Chapter 5 for detailed discussion of the new academic calendars.

cause man no longer lives in an Anglo-American world, the last two semesters will be Western Man Encounters the Non-Western World.

Makeup of lecture teams for each unit varies according to course content. Content of the core courses changes from year to year as some problems become more pressing, others less vital. The only thing that is stable in the program, Young said, is the basic structure. Young has found, in his work with core programs over the years, that students generally do much better in integrative courses than in conventional discipline courses.

Besides avoiding fragmentation of knowledge, the core program has an intent of drawing together the usually separate worlds of scientists on the one hand and humanists–social scientists on the other.

"Not that we'll come together," said Young, "but at least we might gain an appreciation for each other and realize that we deal with the same kinds of problems."

There will be no more Freshman Composition at Baker. The college students should already have mastered composition skills, Young stated firmly. A remedial course will remain in the curriculum for those who have not.

The core curriculum appears to be designed for decidedly bright and eager students. Young grants that it is the kind of program "which good students flock to," but, he said, "it's also the kind of program that should be beneficial to any student because everyone has to face certain basic problems."

The stress on thinking creatively and on taking positions means that even a poor student can profit from the curriculum, according to Young.

The new Baker program cuts required general education courses by roughly one-third. No more will students have to take separate basic courses in religion and philosophy, fine arts, history of civilization, literature, the social world, biological world, physical world, and hygiene.

The only general education requirements beyond the six core courses will be two semesters of interdisciplinary science (physics, chemistry, and biology), two years of foreign language, and two years of physical education.

Requirements for graduation will no longer be in terms of hours, but, more simply, thirty-two academic course units plus four interterms. (Students will take four courses a semester rather than the present average of five.)

At Baker, each department is restructuring its offerings and weeding out esoteric courses. Most of the faculty will be involved in the core curriculum.

Each teaching team will meet biweekly before the program starts and weekly once it is under way. "The two lecturers for the week will tell, point by point, what they plan to say, and we'll tear it apart. In this way, we'll help each other and shape the course," Young explained.

The Baker University program reflects several curricular developments that are being introduced in a growing number of liberal arts colleges—interdisciplinary courses, honors programs, freshman seminars, and independent study. In addition, a growing number of colleges have attempted to resolve curricular issues through manipulation of the academic calendar (discussed in detail in Chapter 5).

Interdisciplinary Approaches

The developing interest in organizing courses along interdisciplinary lines has taken many forms. One is the broad interdisciplinary or interdepartmental major touching a number of areas. Colleges such as San Francisco State have made it possible for a student to go outside his department and organize an interdepartmental major to meet his special circumstances. Springfield College in Massachusetts has what they call a Major and Studies Program. The Majors provide for specialization consistent with professional and graduate demands, and include community leadership, sociology-anthropology, history, and political science–economics. The Studies Program consists of courses from several academic fields which provide a focus for professional preparation. Interdisciplinary research, independent study, and field studies are promoted within the Studies Program which includes Youth Studies, Community Studies, American Studies, and International Studies. In the College of Arts and Letters of Michigan State University, undergraduate programs are offered in American studies, classical studies, comparative literature, Far Eastern and Russian studies, and humanities.

Other colleges have cut across departmental lines in attempting to restructure courses in the sciences, social sciences, humanities, and mathematics by moving away from descriptive treatment of separate subjects in the direction of combinations which seek to establish base structures for fields.

An example of this is the interdepartmental course at the College of Sciences of the University of Santa Clara called A Tri-logue; Atheism, Materialism or Religion. The course combines the disciplines of philosophy, theology, psychology, and sociology in an attempt to deal with the question, "What relevance, if any, does materialism, atheism, and religion have to human truth?"

The College of Arts and Sciences of Wisconsin State University at River Falls has a nonlaboratory course in Great Ideas in Science. The course, open to third-term juniors or seniors, has the following objectives:

1. To show the relationship between the sciences of a period and the intellectual, cultural, and/or religious beliefs of a period.

2. To show that progress in one area of science is dependent on progress in other fields of science.

3. To show how the explosion of scientific knowledge accompanied by the ever-shortening interval between discovery and application of discovery has resulted in many problems.

The main objectives of the course are to help students come to understand the problems man faces and to realize that so many of the decisions which must be made involve value judgments and that they should be made as intelligently as possible by all people—not by just a small segment of the population. The instructors of the course hope to help the student "get over his fear of science, to help him learn which questions to ask and where to get information before he makes a decision." The topics covered in the course include: The Scientific Method, Historical Background, Evolution, Structure of Matter, Energy, Origin of Life, Applications, Control of Science, Conservation and Environmental Control, Population Explosion and Food Supply, and Deoxyribonucleic Acid.

Another interdisciplinary approach which has been frequently attempted is an integrating course or seminar to help students bring together the various strands of their collegiate experience. An early example of this was the senior course at the University of Chicago which was generally well regarded and received. Andrews University in Michigan, in the fall of 1968, introduced a senior course required of all seniors known as Senior Seminar in Contemporary Issues. As the name implies, students exchange ideas and spend some time in relating what they have learned to the issues of the day. The course has a coordinator appointed by the dean, with other professors serving on the teaching team. The course carries five credits and each section of the course is limited to twenty-five to thirty-five students. The course engages the senior in an analysis of the contribution his discipline or any discipline might make toward meeting one or several or all of the following problems: selfishness, crime, war, poverty, racial prejudice, sexual irresponsibility, sickness, family instability, scarcity of food, and natural disasters.

Humboldt State College in California experimented last year with an interdisciplinary senior seminar, Senior Synthesis. The course was intended for better students, but was not restricted to honor students. The course was taught by one person, not by a team. This posed an enormous task of in-depth preparation for the instructor but the faculty felt that having one instructor prevented fragmentation and stimulated an atmosphere of continuing discovery and development of ideas in both class discussion and individual conferences of students with the instructor. The course met once a week and was limited to fifteen students.

The Educational Policies Committee at Illinois College is working on an interdisciplinary capstone course for seniors. It has not been perfect nor has it received approval of the faculty, but quite likely within another year the college will introduce an interdisciplinary course pulling together the liberal arts aspects of the total college experience. The plans are to center the course around certain major problems of the nation, such as freedom, pollution, and the like.

Other areas in which colleges are introducing interdisciplinary approaches are in the humanities and in non-Western studies. In 1964 Cornell College, Iowa, initiated a four-semester course in the humanities for all sophomore and junior students. The course is interdisciplinary, the student having classes with professors of history, philosophy, literature, art, music, religion, and drama. Material for the humanities program consists of the great literature and ideas of man, and the classic works of art and drama. Cornell College faculty members in the humanities area teach and lecture before several small sections of each sophomore and junior class. Their presentations are supplemented by a series of general lectures given by distinguished scholars from American universities throughout the country. Completion of the sophomore-junior studies program in the humanities is a graduation requirement for all Cornell students. The College of Saint Benedict in Minnesota this past year offered two four-credit courses entitled Man's Search for Meaning—the Arts, and Man's Search for Meaning—Literature. After the experience with these two courses the faculty decided to experiment further and interrelate the arts, literature, philosophy, and theology. The theme will continue to be Man's Search for Meaning. The College of Arts and Sciences of Florida State University, Lincoln University in Pennsylvania, Otterbein College, Case Western Reserve, and Findlay College in Ohio, and the College of Arts and Letters at Michigan State University are a few of the colleges offering interdisciplinary humanities courses.

In the area of non-Western studies, Central Michigan University has a program called Interdisciplinary Area Studies Program on Developing Nations, concerned with the general problems of the developing nations of the world today, and offering a minor at the undergraduate level with a special certificate in one of the selected geographical areas. Mills College, California, has developed an interdisciplinary course called Styles of Civilization, which has been described by one of the professors who taught the course, both as "an effective introduction to non-Western Studies and as an innovating approach to interdisciplinary education." Students at Simpson College, Iowa, are required to take either The Civilization of East Asia, or The Civilization of South Asia. The major purpose of these courses is to study a non-Western cultural area in an interdisciplinary manner in an attempt to understand its traditional culture, the impact of the West on this culture, its struggle for independence, and its resultant economic, social, and political problems. Geographical, historical, sociological, anthropological, religious, philosophical, and political elements are part of the two courses. Illinois College has a program of Asian Studies which includes a number of disciplines. Michigan State University designates a very limited number of undergraduate interdisciplinary courses, and credits earned in these may be counted toward a major in a number of cooperating departments. An example is IDC 390, Survey of Subsaharan Africa. The course introduces Africa through integration of the approaches of several disciplines in the social sciences and humanities. Cooperating departments are anthropology, geography, history, political science, and sociology. The course is administered by the geography department.

Ohio University's College of Arts and Sciences currently has two area studies programs, Africa and Southeast Asia, and is planning a Latin American studies program, all using the interdisciplinary approach; the College of Arts and Sciences of the University of Nebraska has a new interdisciplinary major in Latin American Studies; the College of Liberal Arts at Bowling Green State University, Kentucky, offers an interdisciplinary International Studies Major for careers in foreign affairs.

Another area for the introduction of the interdisciplinary approach is found in urban studies. The College of Arts and Science of New York University has a program called Metropolitan Leadership, "a special interdisciplinary curriculum, for a small group of students." The brochure on the program states:

It is a premise of the Program that the institutional leader needs more than a particular professional competence. He will need "a competence beyond the competence." This extra competence has two major characteristics. First the leader must have an unusually broad sensitivity to matters outside his own professional concerns. Secondly, the institutional leader must possess a sometimes quite extraordinary ability to confront and analyze the endless stream of problems that will come across his desk. These problems, in today's world will be complex. Very few of them will be susceptible to solution by the mere application of the particular professional competence which the leader himself happens to possess. The problems of modern urban living are almost always, to put it in a single word, "interdisciplinary."

Springfield College, Massachusetts, offers a program in Urban Life, a program designed to prepare persons to function effectively in dealing with the problems and opportunities of our urban community. The curriculum is interdisciplinary, utilizing the basic resources of all the social sciences and the concepts of social welfare and community development that impinge on the solving of community problems.

Interdisciplinary studies have a long history at Union College, New York. Back in the 1950's the college received a special grant from the Carnegie Foundation to develop what were called ID courses, cutting across the traditional boundaries and relating materials from several disciplines in a special course offered primarily as an elective or distribution requirement. These courses died in the later 1950's. When in 1966–67 the faculty adopted a new program of general education known as Comprehensive Education, it stipulated that the middle-year options should be interdisciplinary and topical. Extending through the four years of college, Comprehensive Education seeks by selective investigation to illustrate how knowledge is interrelated and how the various modes of rational inquiry are applied, both in the academic disciplines and in life itself. All students study the same topics in freshman and senior seminars. During the sophomore and junior years, Comprehensive Education is continued in "options," courses covering a variety of questions but using the same techniques of investigation.

The new curriculum in Amherst College, Massachusetts, which went into effect in the fall of 1966, introduced three one-semester interdepartmental courses called Problem of Inquiry, one each in the humanities, social sciences, and natural sciences. Replacing the former core curriculum as distinctive, common elements of the "Amherst experience," the new courses will be required of all students during the freshman or sophomore year. Their common concern and focus is the nature of disciplines inquiry and the methods by which unordered material can be organized.

A Sloan Foundation grant to Hope College, Michigan, in January 1967, made it possible for the natural science division of the college to reexamine its curriculum. The original intent of the writers of the Sloan Proposal was to devise interdisciplinary courses in science and mathematics to be taken in common by all science majors in the freshman, sophomore, and part of the junior years. In October 1967, the college invited seventeen scientists familiar with interdisciplinary programs to the campus for a Conference on Interdisciplinary Curricula in the Natural

Sciences in the Liberal Arts College. After evaluation of the conference, it was obvious to the faculty that laminated courses have succeeded only so long as they held the enthusiasm of a small group of faculty members. If the support of this small group of scientists waned, the courses were invariably doomed to failure. In addition, the Sloan Committee was convinced that most interdisciplinary courses were very expensive to maintain because of heavy commitment of faculty time to the enterprise and the relatively low election rate by students.

The Sloan Committee of Hope College felt they could meet their pedagogical goal, that is, to demonstrate the unity of the natural sciences to a beginning student, and still maintain departmental structure and integrity by judicious sequencing and restructuring of the introductory courses.

Colleges around the country are also concerned about proper organizational structures which would encourage interdisciplinary approaches as well as innovation. On November 10, 1965, approximately twenty-five members of La Salle College, Pennsylvania, met to discuss plans for establishing an organization designed to promote interdisciplinary projects of "a creative and original nature." In subsequent meetings, the tenor of thinking began to favor the establishment of an institute. The institute was established and ultimately its title became the Institute for Interdisciplinary Studies. Thirty-five faculty members have submitted curriculum vitae, a requisite for joining the institute, and at least twenty others have indicated that they will also become members when they have completed other professional work now in progress. According to the director of the institute,

> The rationale and justification behind planning has always been the constantly reinforced belief that American higher education has not always been adequate to the problem faced by the world outside the walls of the academe. A renascence is desperately needed, and it should be reflected both in the curricular structure of the college as well as in the kind of professional activity engaged in by a school's faculty resources.

In the spring of 1967, the College of Liberal Arts of the University of Minnesota voted to accept an *Ad Hoc* Committee Report which restructured the college's interdisciplinary programs in social science and humanities. The purpose of the reorganization was to establish administrative arrangements which would make possible effective staffing and management of undergraduate interdisciplinary courses or course sequences. In addition, it was hoped that the restructuring would encourage innovation and experimentation in the development of undergraduate instruction as well as establish arrangements which would facilitate appointment to the college faculty of distinguished scholars and teachers whose contributions were outside the disciplinary structure of any single department of the college. The committee reasoned that present administrative arrangements for interdisciplinary programs in social science and the humanities provided little more than an academic "half-life" for faculty members with a commitment to interdisciplinary instruction. Moreover, present arrangements were so cumbersome as to place an excessive burden of conference, argument, and negotiation on faculty members who were associated either directly or indirectly with the program.

The *Ad Hoc* Committee started with the assumption that the College of Liberal Arts should encourage study and instruction based on synthesis of knowledge, or instructional perspectives which may not be comfortably located within any one of the established departments. Given this assumption, the committee concluded that it was "clearly desirable to provide administrative arrangements which will guarantee the quality of such study and instruction, while at the same time minimizing the administrative overburden placed on their conduct."

The committee recognized that the departmental structure of the College of Liberal Arts was well suited to promote the ends of effective specialized instruction but ill suited to foster innovations which would better serve the needs of students working outside an area of specialization, or to develop innovative syntheses of knowledge. In order to achieve the purposes of the restructuring, the following administrative structure was recommended and adopted:

1.   The program would be the direct responsibility of the associate dean for humanities, who would serve as chairman of a Program Advisory Committee of five members. These five members shall include four senior faculty members from the *departments represented in the Humanities Divisional Council,* plus the program director serving *ex officio.* The four senior faculty members should be appointed by the dean with the concurrence of the *CLA Educational Policy Committee.* At least two of these four members shall be persons not currently teaching in the program. Among the duties of the Program Advisory Committee should be continuous review *and evaluation* of the program curriculum, and of the major sequence of courses.

2.   The program director shall be appointed by the dean with the concurrence of the *CLA Educational Policy Committee,* upon recommendation from the associate dean and the members of his program advisory committee other than the program director. The program director should be appointed for a term of not more than three years, with reap-

pointment possible. Should the need arise for additional administrative personnel for the management of the program, the associate dean and his advisory committee shall make such recommendation to the dean.

3. The associate dean and the program advisory committee would have the discretionary power to initiate any course or course sequence at any time subject only: (*a*) to the concurrence of the dean; (*b*) to establishment of procedures for evaluating the contributions of the course or course sequence in question; (*c*) approval of the College Curriculum Review Committee; and (*d*) stipulation of a specific period of time, not to exceed three years, at the end of which the course or sequence could either be discontinued, or submitted to the full divisional council for the processing usual to proposals for adding new courses to the curriculum.

4. The College Curriculum Review Committee shall also be empowered to pass upon innovative, experimental courses proposed by departments, to be taught in the departments or in the program, using the same criteria of judgment as in item 3 above. The intent of this provision is to allow for more flexible, rapid, and experimental departmental and interdepartmental curricular changes.

5. The associate dean with the concurrence of the program advisory committee would have the power to recommend to the dean the appointment of either visiting or permanent professors of the college. Approval for such proposed appointments would be limited to persons whose qualifications as scholars and teachers are outstanding, and who could be expected to serve most effectively in forwarding the interdisciplinary purposes of the college.

6. The presumption is that persons teaching in the programs will be drawn from the departments, either by joint arrangements, or by purchase of teaching time from the departments. However, if in exceptional cases the appropriate associate dean and his advisory committee recommend a particular core appointee for a given program, and if this recommendation is approved by the *CLA Educational Policy Committee,* such an appointment should be possible.

The administrative structure for the Social Science Program would parallel that for the Humanities Program. The Committee on Interdisciplinary and Interdepartmental Programs felt that there was merit in a proposal for the reorganization of the Natural Science Program parallel to that proposed for the Social Sciences and Humanities Programs.

There is mixed reaction to the use of the interdisciplinary approach in curricular revision. The academic dean of St. Augustine's College in North Carolina, in commenting on the required course in humanities which involves the members of the departments of English and music and art, indicates that

a great number of advantages have accrued in strengthening this program by such an interdisciplinary approach. Primarily, it has enabled the students to hear scholars from the various disciplines present material pertinent to the aims and objectives of the course. Because of the diversity of materials presented, such a presentation would be less effective if it were handled by one department alone.

The dean also saw disadvantages, the major one involving the scheduling of persons from the various departments to participate in the course.

Because of class assignments in their own departments, quite often it is somewhat difficult to arrange a schedule in which persons from other departments may give lectures, demonstrations, and discussions at a time when the Humanities course is meeting. Largely, this problem has been resolved by use of several persons from a given department, thereby alleviating the necessity of requiring one individual to be on hand at all times in the Humanities course from a given department.

The faculty at Luther College, Iowa, are convinced that interdisciplinary studies are of great value, both to the students and to the faculty. The head of the religion department of Luther College stated that:

We have just begun in this area, and we will be doing very much more along these lines in the future. Such studies help both students and faculty to see the artificiality of the lines between the disciplines, serve to bring down the barriers, and help to develop more consistent standpoints toward both life and learning. Moreover, they seem to create more interest than the ordinary courses.

On the other hand, Kenneth R. Walker, assistant dean of Arkansas Polytechnic College, commenting on their interdisciplinary courses in American studies, humanities, and a problems course listed in the departments of sociology, economics, and political science, points out several disadvantages.

First, it is very difficult to obtain faculty members who can make the type of integration of American history and American literature required in this course. If one attempts to break up the course and have specialists in American history and American literature teach their particular disciplines, the course tends to lose its integration. True integration in a course, if it is to be truly beneficial to the students, must originate in the instructor's mind. In addition, the course covers a great bulk of material which is very difficult to cover adequately in the six hours allotted to it. What I have said about American Studies generally also applies to the Humanities courses. . . . The problems course has even more problems in integration than the others. . . . In our experience it has also usually been difficult to obtain superior students for this class. The capable student has either shied away from the course because of the apparent complex nature of the course or else he does not have the background required to take a course which embodies the disciplines of economics, sociology, and political science.

Despite all the practical problems in teaching and administering the interdisciplinary courses, Dean Walker indicates that "I still believe that they are well worth the effort. Like most ideals, however, they fall short in implementation."

John E. Horner, president of Hanover College, Indiana, feels that there is considerable difference in the success of interdisciplinary studies at Hanover College, an unevenness which he feels is likewise true at other institutions. Horner feels that the "blend" of instructors makes quite a difference in the success or failure of the program. He believes it is important to identify those persons in various departments who are committed to interdisciplinary studies and are willing to work effectively and well with others, and says:

Although we cannot support this view with concrete data, it is our impression that the people who are most successful in this area are individuals with the broadest interests and a willingness to express this interest through the lecture process. The "withdrawn specialist" is most unhappy working in this context and fights the system rather than supporting it.

Students at Hanover have reacted positively to interdisciplinary studies. President Horner suggests that the student reception has been more enthusiastic than that of the faculty. "The desire of faculty to return to their specialized havens where there is greater security," says Horner "is more obvious to us than the negative reaction of students." He maintains firmly that "such studies are very necessary in a small liberal arts college, which theoretically expresses a philosophy that there should be a cross fertilization of the disciplines."

The president of Albright College, Pennsylvania, feels that one of the advantages of interdisciplinary study is the fact that various departments become aware of each other's disciplines because of the dialogue between faculty. He feels that the main disadvantage is pure economics. Sister Maria de Ricci, dean of studies at Rosary College, Illinois, indicates that interdisciplinary courses are generally popular with students and enjoyed by participating faculty. "However, they are expensive courses from the college's point of view," she states, "because they involve the time of several professors, and this is the only disadvantage."

TABLE 2 LIBERAL ARTS COLLEGES INVOLVED WITH CURRICULAR INNOVATIONS

Curriculum Practice	Number of Usable Responses to Item [a]	Percentage of Usable Responses	Before 1961	Percentage of Responses	1961 and After	Percentage of Responses	Planning to Introduce	Percentage of Responses
Interdisciplinary studies	593	67.2	254	42.8	261	44.0	78	13.2
Honors programs	635	72.0	298	46.9	268	42.2	69	10.9
Freshman seminars	314	35.6	73	23.2	179	57.0	62	19.8
Independent study for superior students only	580	65.8	259	44.7	287	49.4	34	5.9
Independent study for all students	293	33.2	118	40.3	133	45.4	42	14.3
Non-Western studies	497	56.3	173	34.8	258	51.9	66	13.3
Undergraduate study abroad	561	63.6	217	38.7	281	50.1	63	11.2
Off-campus study in the United States	283	32.1	119	42.1	122	43.1	42	14.8
Work-study programs	479	54.3	89	18.6	370	77.2	20	4.2
Community service projects	620	70.3	246	39.7	341	55.0	33	5.3

[a] The total number of usable responses to the questionnaire was 882.

Lebanon Valley College in Pennsylvania recently abandoned their program of interdisciplinary courses in the freshman and sophomore years but have begun a study of interdisciplinary programs at the upper level. Perhaps Associate Dean Archer Jones of the College of Arts and Science of the University of South Carolina best reflects the state of interdisciplinary studies on many liberal arts college campuses in the country. "I fear," said Dean Jones, "that the present interdisciplinary studies here are mostly hope rather than reality."

HONORS PROGRAMS

A great deal of attention has been given in recent years to the special needs of the abler or superior student. Of particular note are the many developments in the use of special honors courses and seminars within the framework of a total honors program. An early manifestation of the honors program was the creation of the Pass–Honors degree at Swarthmore in 1922, but as an important movement it did not gain headway until the American public, prompted by Russian scientific achievements, climaxed by Sputnik in 1957, demanded greater rigor in education. Honors programs are intended for the intellectually gifted, with many of the honors courses broad rather than disciplinary. They stress important questions and raise value issues. Honors courses clearly seek to place work in a broad context and to help students establish relationships between their lives and what they study.

The Western Washington State College Honors Program for lower-division honors students was formally inaugurated in 1960. The program was subsequently extended to upper-division work and honors opportunities are available from college entrance to college graduation. Honors courses include tutorials, colloquia, and departmental honors courses. Beginning with his first year in the program, each student is assigned a faculty tutor who acts as counselor or academic advisor. The tutor meets regularly with the student on a one-to-one basis. Together they decide on the content and direction of the tutorial. The tutor assigns readings and papers and these form the discussion basis for subsequent meetings. As a rule, honors students write five thousand or more words each quarter for the tutorial and colloquium together.

All honors students participate in colloquia, informal evening meetings of about a dozen students and a faculty member, during which discussion in depth centers on a vital idea or set of ideas. Colloquia are organized under the general headings of science, social science, and humanities. Beginning with the junior year, the emphasis shifts "from the romance of dealing with exciting, provocative ideas to the precision of disciplinary rigor," and most honors work is undertaken within departments. Much of the student's upper-division tutorial work is devoted to his honors thesis which in many cases proves to be of a quality equivalent to the usual master's thesis. The college bears the cost of the final typing and binding of theses.

Several privileges are extended to honors students. Each year a publication, *Honors Papers,* presents the best honors work as judged by faculty and student editors. An Honors Lounge and Library is reserved for their use. They are the guests of the college at an annual honors banquet at which a cash award is given to the outstanding honors student. And at least quarterly, the Honors Board provides a guest lecturer of note who addresses honors students and invited faculty.

Western's Honors Program is administered by an Honors Board charged with responsibility for developing and coordinating appropriate programs, planning future phases of the program, selecting students for the program, and approving students' college work, including graduation "With Honors." The Honors Board receives suggestions from faculty and honors students alike and, with representatives of the latter, meets in joint session at least quarterly.

Honors students are selected from recommendations of high school faculty and counselors, from scores on college entrance examinations, from previous performance, and from volunteers who meet these requirements. Retention in the program is by performance as assessed by tutors, college faculty, and the Honors Board.

The Honors Program at the College of Arts and Sciences of the University of Vermont is designed for "the superior student with unusual initiative and intellectual curiosity, and provides an opportunity to pursue a special project without the restrictions of the classroom routine." Such a student enters a program of reading, research, or creation under the direction of the department of his choice. A student may take honors in either the junior or senior year, or both. To be eligible a student must have a general average of 85 in his sophomore year and have the permission of the chairman of the department in which he wishes to take honors. Students seeking senior honors must apply before the end of the junior year to the department concerned and to the Committee on Honors. Applicants must be able to complete graduation requirements by the end of the senior year. They need a general average of at least 85 for the work of the last two years. Candidates must present a satisfactory written report and pass an oral examination on the general field in which honors are sought. On the basis of a written report, the oral examination, and the department recommendation, the Committee on Honors may recommend to the dean the award of Senior Honors on completion of all requirements for graduation.

At Morris Harvey College in West Virginia, the Honors Program is planned to include each of the student's four years. The first-year student substitutes the Honors English in lieu of the regular Freshman English course. Emphasis is placed on reading from key thinkers and writers with a seminar atmosphere prevailing. The second year is devoted to an investigation of the social sciences, again in place of the core curriculum course in social science. In addition to the readings and discussion, the upper-division students present a public colloquium each semester in which each discusses briefly some aspect of the material covered in class. According to Henry Wolf, chairman of the Honors Program,

the program has been successful. The enthusiasm of the students has been continually manifest and while all are not particularly vocal in class, they have voiced in private their appreciation of the opportunities such a course offers. Absences from class are practically nonexistent. The courses have even had beneficial effects upon the professors, stimulating them and serving as the highlight of the teaching load.

Bellarmine College in Kentucky uses what they call Cardinal Section, a term which serves both as a name for an Honors Program within the college and as a description of a core of courses limited in enrollment to gifted students invited to participate in an experience designed to "excite and reward heightened intellectual effort." The chief features of this program are to be found in the intensified course work, offered to small groups with especially selected instructors, and in various related academic and cultural activities. Students are enrolled in the Cardinal Sections only by invitation. Selection is made after consideration of entrance test scores, high school records, personal recommendations, and an interview. Twenty students as a maximum are chosen for the program each year.

Most honors programs follow the aforementioned patterns. During the academic year 1962–63, the University of North Carolina extended its Honors Program from departmental study undertaken only by seniors to all four undergraduate years. The full four-year program was developed within the framework of the following goals:

1.   To identify able students early in their college careers and to encourage them to move ahead as rapidly as possible and in as many paths as natural talent and energy will permit.

2.   To promote an interest in academic work and in the academic

life by providing opportunities for closer contact with the faculty and with visiting distinguished scholars.

3. To encourage students to plan for graduate work and possible careers in college teaching. To accomplish this objective, a special advising staff has been established for freshman and sophomore honors students. One objective of this staff is to encourage honors students to acquire in their undergraduate years tools such as foreign languages and statistics which are required for graduate study. Standards of eligibility for the program as well as evaluation procedures are the same as at the colleges previously mentioned.

The Departmental and Interdisciplinary Honors Program adopted by the faculty of Macalester College, Minnesota, in the spring of 1966 illustrates the various groups involved in such a program as well as the role each plays. At Macalester, the Honors Committee has the following duties:

1. The committee admits students into the program.
2. Near the beginning of each school year, the committee devises the detailed administrative program for the year (such as deadline dates) and transmits this information to the departmental chairmen.
3. The committee advises the faculty on those policy matters relating to the program which require faculty action.
4. An annual report is given to the faculty on the operation and accomplishments of the program, and reports are made at other times, as necessary.
5. The committee will continuously evaluate the operation of the program and recommend changes to improve the program.
6. The committee is the final judge in disagreements about the propriety of honors courses, basic departmental honors programs and the individual programs of students, and standard of accomplishment in the program.

The duties of the department are:

1. To devise and staff an attractive departmental Honors Program.
2. To encourage all qualified students to enter the Program.
3. To assist, guide and encourage students as necessary, to strive for excellence in the Honors Program.
4. To administer all parts of the program dealing directly with the Honors students; recommend the outside examiners to the Dean; and manage the details of the senior Honors comprehensive and thesis examinations, including notification of the registrar of the examiner's recommendations.
5. To recommend action to the registrar for students who drop out of the

program or fail to receive a recommendation for Honors from the outside examiner. In particular, to determine the equivalent between the nature and quality of the Honors work done by the student, and acceptable pass work toward a regular degree.

The outside examiner composes and evaluates the senior honors comprehensive examination, determines the quality of the project or thesis, and conducts an oral defense or explanation of the honors project or thesis. The comprehensive examination may be written, oral, or both, according to the desire of the examiner. In addition, the examiner determines the award, but may consult with the department members about the standards of accomplishment that are expected of honors candidates. If the department staff disagrees with the evaluation of the examiner, final determination is made by vote of the Honors Committee on the basis of evidence presented to it.

The dean of the college is the administrative director of the Honors Program, being responsible for those duties which are not specifically detailed to the Honors Committee and the department chairmen. The dean coordinates the individuals and groups involved in the program and his office maintains the permanent records of the Honors Program. The dean's office manages the clerical details of operating the program, such as inviting outside examiners, arranging seminars and banquets, or circularizing honors candidates or thesis supervisors.

At Macalester, honors candidates are excused from all attendance requirements but are not thereby excused from responsibility for course requirements. The granting of the degree *cum laude, magna cum laude,* or *summa cum laude* is determined entirely by the grade-point average prerequisites set by the faculty, and requires no additional kind of accomplishment. The Honors Program has special course and examination requirements, and departmental honors are not dependent on some minimum grade-point average at the time of graduation. They are conferred for satisfactory completion only of the Honors Program, not for some general level of attainment. The recipient of the degree with departmental honors may or may not also graduate *cum laude, magna cum laude,* or *summa cum laude.*

Albion College in Michigan, Cornell College in Iowa, High Point College in North Carolina, the College of Liberal Arts of Syracuse University in New York all have honors programs which illustrate the essential features of honors programs throughout the country. Liberal arts college honors programs try to identify as "honor students" young men and women who are both able and willing to do independent and imaginative thinking. A major purpose that runs throughout the honors programs is to provide educational opportunities for the exceptionally well-endowed student whose goal may be a more intensive intellectual development than that of the average student. In 1967, for example, the College of Liberal Arts at Wayne State University in Michigan carefully scrutinized the records of over 1,200 prospective freshmen. Out of these, 200 were invited for interviews. The end result was the admission of 43 entering freshmen to the Honors Program. The Honors Program at William Carey College, Mississippi, is designed for students who are valedictorians or salutatorians and others who rank in the top 5 per cent of their high school graduating classes.

Honors courses are different in other important ways. The classes are small and are conducted with more than usual freedom and informality. Memorization as such receives less emphasis; instead, students are expected to discover meaning and order and relationships among the facts they have learned. Students have opportunities to establish close relationships with faculty members upon whom they can try out their ideas. Sometimes they work in pairs or in small groups on projects of mutual interest. Withal, they learn that education is a collaborative venture in which both students and instructors share responsibilities.

FRESHMAN SEMINARS

Paralleling developments in the use of interdisciplinary studies as well as independent study, a growing number of colleges employ or plan to adopt seminar-type programs during the freshman year. These programs seek to provide the student with an experience in depth at the very beginning of his college career, as contrasted with the large-size, broad, survey-type courses in which he frequently finds himself during his first year in college. For instance, in the fall of 1965, Antioch College, Ohio, inaugurated an experimental program for freshmen. The program, on which Antioch planners worked for about two years, deals with the very problems against which students on many campuses raise their voices and banners—the problems of anonymity, generalization vs. specialization, and rigidity of curriculum.

To deal with the student's feeling of anonymity during his first year at college, Antioch provides each with a home base within the institution, a faculty preceptor. To meet the problem of specialization-generalization and the variety of approaches to learning needed for students with varied interests, goals, and high school preparation, Antioch dispenses with organized freshman general education courses. Instead, each major academic area has agreed on some of the most important questions sixteen-to eighteen-year-olds ask about the humanities, the social sciences, the physical sciences. The answers will be available in many forms. It is up to each student, with his preceptor's help, to decide what he is interested in learning and what he must learn to qualify for second-year standing, and how to get both. Each area, for instance, offers from twenty to sixty core presentations that show the interrelationships of academic departments while maintaining disciplinary integrity. Presentations contain the main concepts of a department that faculty believe students should be familiar with. Thus a student who wants some history but is familiar with the Greek-Persia-Rome period may skip those presentations in favor of a series on the Rise and Fall of Christendom with which he is unfamiliar.

From each eighty-minute presentation, two to five seminars of varying duration spin off. Some are designed for students who already have chosen a major field; others for those whose achievement test scores indicate more work in an area or specific subject is needed to qualify for advanced courses; still others for those who elect to follow a personal interest. And to encourage freshmen to risk new or previously troublesome subjects, to enroll in a seminar with a "tough" instructor, and to partake of as many academic offerings and community government activities as time and talent warrant, the college has dispensed with grades. Instead, student and preceptor, who together have been measuring his progress toward stated goals every two weeks, will decide, at the end of the year, what second-year work he is qualified for.

As might be expected, faculty reaction to the program runs the gamut from those who believe Antioch students are bright enough to learn under any circumstances to those who hail the new approach to general education as revolutionary. But many will agree with President James P. Dixon that the new program is "simply one more attempt to involve the Antioch student in the design, conduct, and evaluation of his own education," and to meet the students' expectation that "college will help them enter society in constructive ways earlier."

Other colleges had experimented with new approaches to teaching freshmen quite early. An example is Lawrence University, Wisconsin, where a course called Freshman Studies was established in 1945. Nathan M. Pusey, president of Harvard University, was president of Lawrence College from 1944 until June of 1953 and is credited with originating the program. Pusey had already been experimenting with such a course as a member of the faculty of Wesleyan University. When Pusey first proposed such a course to a group of faculty representatives from all departments at Lawrence College, he tried to define what appeared to him to be most needed by freshmen entering college. Some kind of course, he believed, should be devised for first-year students that would be entirely different in nature and scope from anything encountered in high school, not, of course, simply as a novelty, but as a means to awaken them intellectually as early as possible. It was never his contention that this awakening could not take place in any course, but the fact that it so often did not occur until later in the student's career, if at all, seemed to suggest the advisability of experimenting with a new course required of all freshmen. The Freshmen Studies course is required of all freshmen enrolled at Lawrence. As one of the four academic courses which make up a full program for the first-year student, it has been substituted for a previously required course in Freshman English. It carries four hours' credit each semester and meets four times a week. At least three of these meetings are held in small groups of fourteen to sixteen for discussion of the readings. For students who are considered below the standard of college freshmen in grammar, punctuation, and spelling, an afternoon laboratory of two hours a week is provided. The feature of the course which has created the most interest, and consternation as well, is the composition of the teaching staff. The discussion leaders are teachers drawn from almost every department of the college; and in the Freshman Studies course all the teachers teach all the books, not merely those from the field of their specialty. The student understands that each of his teachers is a specialist in some one field but is interested, as an educated man or woman, in other fields. The student learns that liberally educated people are able to read significant books on various subjects with intelligence and pleasure without, of course, pretending to be specialists in them. He also learns that variously trained individuals bring to books various insights and that great books have many implications and may be read in many ways. Ideally, according to the vice president, there should be a system of rotation within the faculty "to ensure a more equitable distribution of the labors and benefits of Freshman Studies."

The Harvard College Freshman Seminar Program, introduced in 1959, was conceived with several purposes in mind:

1. To sustain the focused commitments which some students appear to bring with them,
2. To provide immediately for students of all kinds vivid and challenging introduction to some significant area of study,
3. To give the student a sense of engagement in the life of the university, and
4. To provide students in the freshman year better opportunity for intelligent decisions in determining their departmental concentration.[4]

[4] Bryon Stookey, Jr., *The Freshman Seminar Program: A Report to the Faculty of Arts and Science,* February 1963.

During the years from 1959 to 1963, more than eleven hundred Harvard and Radcliffe freshmen, or about one-fifth of the combined freshmen classes, participated in 130 seminars.[5] With regard to method it is possible to distinguish, in general, three types of seminars. One type was designed to provide "committed" freshmen early experience of advanced and adult work within a specialized field. A second type examined the nature of a broad area of inquiry by treating in depth a sharply focused but representative subject. The late Clyde Kluckhohn's seminar on the Navajo Indian was an enterprise of this kind. Finally, there have been some seminars that set out to demonstrate the nature of a wide area by considering broad questions from the start. Such were the seminars directed by David Riesman, which ranged through literature, philosophy, anthropology, and psychology to study the relation of the individual to society.

The typical seminar has engaged from eight to ten freshmen in a common inquiry, drawing increasingly on individual, independent work as the inquiry's context and shape gained clarity. All have sought, through a serious intellectual enterprise, to associate freshmen in a close, provocative way with an interested scholar.

In March 1963, freshman seminars were established on a permanent basis at Harvard. Students have repeatedly said that their freshman seminar was the major intellectual experience of their first year. The majority of faculty members who have conducted seminars have been enthusiastic and believe in the program. They utilized the seminar method to experiment with innovations in the teaching of freshmen, and many of them conducted extraordinarily successful experiments.

Many colleges use the Freshman Seminar as part of the core approach for all students. In 1967, for example, the Lindenwood College faculty developed the Freshman Common Course. The course grew gradually out of a multitude of discussions and suggestions involving almost everyone on the faculty. According to James F. Hood, assistant dean of Lindenwood College, Missouri,

We wanted to meet several problems at once. The first of these was the cry of this generation for "relevance." We wanted a course that would speak to and about the prevailing problems of our day—a course that would jump past the boundaries of the campus. Hence the theme—Dynamics of the Twentieth Century.

The faculty of Lindenwood also realized that a new kind of teacher-student relationship would be needed in such a course. Hood explained,

[5] United States Department of Health, Education, and Welfare, *Approach to Independent Study*. Compiled by Winslow R. Hatch and Alice L. Richards (Washington, D.C.: U.S. Government Printing Office, 1964). p. 11.

If we ask the question, "How can man be so inhuman to his fellows as to create concentration camps and gas chambers," we can have no final answers. It becomes a matter of mutual exploration. We can suggest to students ways to look and methods of checking the results, but we cannot give them the results; we don't have them. But we do know that the search for answers is important. . . . In that sense, the course carries a kind of implicit conviction that before protest and change must come understanding and conviction. To use a familiar analogy, we do not want to indoctrinate students to either swim upstream, drift downstream, or just hang on to the bank and watch. What we do want is that they understand the nature and direction of the river so they can make their own choices about direction intelligently.

In addition, the faculty wanted students to realize the essential unity of knowledge. They felt that the distinguishing mark of the small liberal arts college is that it serves as a mediating factor among the disciplines.

To realize all these goals, the faculty of Lindenwood created a course which they described as "rather like an onion—it has a series of concentric layers, all contributing to each other." The outer layer of the onion is the plenary series. This brings the whole class together to hear a flow of outside people who share with the students and the faculty their special knowledge and feelings about the process of change. To achieve the approach the faculty desired, the old fifty-minute classes were abandoned and Monday and Thursday mornings were set aside for the course. But the real heart of the course is the discussion group. There are nine in all, three social science groups, three humanities groups, and three science groups, with nine faculty to match. Through a rotation system, students experience all three areas during the year. The nine groups, incidentally, are formed around the residence halls. The assistant dean said:

The only major problem of the course was the unexpected conservatism of the students who were unaccustomed to the relatively freewheeling schedule. The lack of specific tasks at the same specific hours each week frightened them a bit. The same is true for some of the faculty. The Director still has to do a bit of "stage managing" to get all the groups to the proper places at the proper times.

Some colleges use the freshman seminar as part of their honors program. Adrian College, Michigan, for instance, has a freshman seminar in English which is also the first year of a four-year honors program. Westmont College, California, has adopted the practice of allowing freshmen to take certain seminars. The freshman must be in an honors group. The freshman seminars in general are courses which the student takes in addition to those normally required of freshmen. Occasionally, as with the freshman seminar in English, they may be substituted for general graduation requirements. Guilford College, North Carolina, offers to approximately fifty students of better than average ability the opportunity of participating in freshman seminars as part of their first-year program. The seminars to be offered each year are carefully selected by a faculty committee from proposals made by faculty members who are prepared to consider with selected groups of not more than fifteen students some challenging topic in which the faculty member has some special interest and competence.

Still other colleges use the freshman seminar as an orientation program. Wittenberg University, Ohio, has a New Student Seminar which they introduced in 1967. The purposes of the seminar are to introduce students immediately to the instructors who make up the Wittenberg faculty and to introduce them to the methods and types of books and ideas which they could expect to encounter throughout their college years. The New Student Seminar takes place during the first week on campus.

The Freshman Seminar at Salem College, North Carolina, is directed by the dean of students. In the first semester freshmen are required to attend a seminar each week. This is a discussion group that is concerned with topics of interest to the freshmen. The course is not for credit and deals with such topics as study habits, group living, liberal education, and the like. In the second semester the freshmen attend what is called Academic Open Houses which means that the freshmen meet with the members of the various departments in order to receive information about the majors, the opportunities for graduate study, and for jobs related to the major.

Earlham College, Indiana, has had freshman seminars for the last three years. The seminars have been received enthusiastically by students and are popular with the faculty. According to Joseph E. Elmore, vice president for academic affairs,

The students have emphasized two advantages in their evaluation of the seminars. The smallness of the class and the opportunity to get to know the faculty member more closely than in any other classes; the opportunity to study a subject other than the typical introductory courses during the freshman year.

Sister Maria de Ricci, dean of studies at Rosary College, Illinois, reflects the general evaluation of freshman seminars when she stated that

we have found that freshmen respond very well to small seminars—the personal challenge, small group discussion methods, independent research, close association with a professor—all are especially formative influences during a student's first year in college.

INDEPENDENT STUDY

The idea that colleges use independent study in their instructional program is, of course, not new. In a 1957 report on independent study programs, Bonthius and his colleagues listed a total of 334 such programs in 256 institutions.[6] (See Table 2.) Independent study has long been regarded as the prerogative of the superior student in honors and tutorial courses. What is new is that in its growing use independent study is becoming available to all students, and further, it is available at the beginning rather than the close of the student's college career. Thus a number of colleges have instituted winter-term, or interim-term, programs of independent study in which all students are expected to take part. A major implication of the new programs is that independent study can be used with a wide range of students. Colleges using independent study are reporting that the fruitful uses of independence may depend quite as much on the character and personality of the student, the nature of the field of study, and the educational goals sought as on the intellectual capacity of the individual student.

There are many forces pressing for the growing use of independence. The shortage of fully qualified teachers, the mounting evidence that mere acquisition of facts and abstract principles is far from enough to produce an educated person, the multiplication of knowledge at overwhelming rates, and the growing conviction that learning is essentially an active rather than a passive process are some of the arguments advanced for the growing development of independent study approaches in liberal arts colleges around the nation. All the evidence suggests that the inevitable effects of the explosion of knowledge, the rapid changes and increased demands of many occupations and professions, and increased leisure will place a premium on the ability to continue the learning process throughout one's active life. If we accept the idea of "lifelong learning," then we must find ways to prepare each student to rely more on himself to learn things for which he has an awakened interest and motivation. There is a good deal of growing evidence that students can assume a greater share of the responsibility for their own learning.

Independent study may occur in a variety of ways. All methods have in common allowing the student to read or do research on his own for varying lengths of time and amounts of credit with a minimum of faculty consultation. For example, at Methodist College, North Carolina, a stu-

[6] Robert H. Bonthius, James F. Davis, and J. Garber Drushal, in collaboration with Francis V. Guille and Warren P. Spencer, *The Independent Study Program in the United States* (New York: Columbia University Press, 1957).

dent who is admitted to an independent study program meets initially with his supervising instructor for a general survey of the material to be covered, bibliographical suggestions, and a general outline of the working assignment for the semester. The student is then required to begin developing his own bibliography and usually to begin work on some particular aspect of the subject material, with the approval of the instructor. The student is encouraged to develop his own topic for research and study and work along the lines of the graduate research programs in universities. During the course of the semester the student is required to hold conferences with his supervising instructor at intervals designated by the instructor. This ranges from one fifty-minute conference a week to biweekly conferences. In no circumstances does an undergraduate go for more than two weeks without a conference with his supervising instructor. Dean Samuel J. Womack indicates that the major disadvantage of the program "is an inordinate amount of time to devote to an individual student in a small college situation, when the teaching load is still rather extensive— 15 semester hours."

Minot State College in North Dakota offers two sets of courses which allow independent study for superior students as well as for the average student. The 400-level course is available to any student with a *B* average or better. Students in these courses are allowed to choose independent study topics and to develop these with what help they need. Minot State also offers independent study for the *C* student in a 200-level course, for as much as two hours each, up to a total of six quarter-hours credit. Tarkio College in Missouri makes a distinction between its Honors Program which is for superior students and its independent study program which is less demanding both with respect to admission and production.

Other practices reported by colleges providing independent study for all students included offering courses which are listed in the catalog as Independent Study, Reading and Research, or Directed Reading. These courses are usually not compulsory but they give the student a chance to study some aspect of a discipline in greater depth than is possible through the formal course offerings. Generally, these courses are open only to juniors and seniors. Hartwick College and Elmira College in New York, Denison University in Ohio, Columbia Union College in Maryland, Bethany College in Kansas, and Southampton College in New York are among the colleges offering this approach. Another approach is that employed by Reed College in Oregon, which gives students in some classes a week or so of independent study. The method is usually reserved for upper-class students.

Sometimes the student, working with films, taped lectures, programmed materials, texts, and assigned readings, is expected to accomplish almost completely on his own the goals usually supported by classroom procedures of lecture and discussion. Oklahoma Christian College, for instance, because of the facilities in their Learning Center, allows students to do more work on their own with taped materials. While this is not independent study in the sense of independent research, it does place more responsibility on the student for his own learning. The use of media and programmed instruction is reviewed in a later section of this chapter.

A number of programs of independent study have sought to make use of small-group or team approaches to independent study. At Illinois College five students majoring in history and five majoring in sociology undertook a joint project dealing with the Negro problem in America. Each of the ten students was assigned, as determined for himself, an area of the problem. The ten, together with the two faculty members, made up a seminar. They got together occasionally to discuss the total problem, and each of the ten students reported to the group his findings with respect to his particular area of research.

One of the most frequently attempted of the emerging experimental patterns in independent study is the "January term," or "winter term," or the "intersemester," as it has come variously to be known. The purposes appear to be similar in all these undertakings. The January term at Florida Presbyterian College, inaugurated in 1960, illustrates how many of the new programs seek to extend the opportunity for independent work to all students. The winter term is a special four-week period interposed between the fall and the spring semesters. Classes are suspended during January, and the students, including freshmen, undertake an independent study or research project. Intended to develop habits and skills for independent work, the program requires each student to undertake a problem growing out of either his own experience or suggestions offered by a professor. He is free to make the choice, and he may also decide whether his project is such that he will work with another student, with a group of students, or by himself. A professor—again, of the student's choosing—remains available for consultation and evaluation throughout the period. Each student is expected to put in about fifty hours a week, and, at the close of the special term, to present the results as a paper, short story, painting, product of a laboratory experiment, or the like. During the freshman and sophomore years, the student is encouraged to select a topic outside his major field of interest; during the junior and senior years, the topic is to be selected from within his field. About two-thirds of the faculty regularly participate in winter term work. The other faculty members are free during this time to carry on their own research and studies.

Similar winter term programs are under way at St. Olaf College and

Macalester College in Minnesota, Colby College in Maine, Bard College in New York, Mercyhurst College in Pennsylvania, and many other colleges either have adopted the practice or are planning to adopt the innovation. St. Olaf's program is the same as the program at Florida Presbyterian College. January Interim at St. Olaf's is a four-week period of intensive study for all students. During interim each student works in a single area. Freshmen meet with their instructors for a minimum of two hours a week during interim. All additional meetings, both group and individual, are left to the instructor. Each student is expected to contribute a minimum of forty hours a week to research and other activity directly pertinent to his subject. Grades are derived from a written or oral examination, an evaluation of a written thesis or project, or by a combination of methods. All students are required to participate in interim during each year of residence at St. Olaf.

The Winter Field Period, one of the distinctive aspects of the Bard College program, is a seven-week term during which students explore vocational, creative, or intellectual interests away from campus and classroom. The field period comes every year between the fall and spring semesters and lasts from the end of Christmas vacation until late February. There are two types of field period: the work-experience project and the reading and/or creative project. In general, freshmen and sophomores take work experience projects; the more advanced students take reading and/or creative projects. Seniors usually spend the seven-week term working on their senior projects.

In September 1967, Mercyhurst College reorganized its academic program and made the focal point of the new curriculum the Intersession, a three-week period of concentrated "study in depth," in a specific area of interest of the student's choice. Each student is required to complete four intersessions in her college career, concentrating on active, independent study under the guidance of a qualified teacher. Freshmen and seniors pursue a topic in the liberal studies curriculum, while sophomores and juniors will study in their field of major concentration. To provide the needed block of time for the intersession, Mercyhurst adopted a three-term calendar year. Each term is ten weeks in length, with the intersession scheduled between Terms I and II.

Allowing students to participate for a semester, a summer, or for some shorter period in an off-campus project under the social or tutorial supervision of a faculty member is another approach used to encourage independent study. Such projects include but are not limited to foreign study, a study of the social or governmental process in a large city, or a study of flora and fauna at some location away from civilization. Kalamazoo

College, Michigan, requires study abroad, as well as career or service experience. Antioch College in Ohio emphasizes work experience. At Goshen College, Indiana, the objectives of their Study-Service Trimester is to examine and experience the culture of another country as well as to participate in giving service to people in need. In addition, it is intended that the student experience an intensive relationship as a part of a small group with one or two faculty members before he decides on his collegiate and vocational goals. The student chooses one of several locations in consultation with the director of the study-service program, and spends one trimester there some time after the end of his freshman year and before the start of his junior year. At each location a small group of students is directed by one or more faculty members who are usually on location for at least three trimesters and direct the academic program and give personal counsel to the students. The student receives credit for three courses for this work. The fee paid by the student is the same for a trimester in residence at the college. Transportation from Goshen to the study-service location is arranged and paid for by the college.

The results of a student's independent study can take a number of tangible forms. The most common is writing a paper based on library research. The conclusion of laboratory or field work sometimes calls for the preparation of a paper. Another concluding requirement may be an oral or written comprehensive examination dealing with the material read or studied. At some schools students must take an examination as well as present a paper on their independent study. Finally, the culmination of individual study in an artistic or creative field may take the form of a work of art or of some appropriate performance.

Completed independent study projects are sometimes awarded letter grades and treated like any other course in compiling the student's grade-point average. More often, however, these projects are judged on the basis of Pass/Fail or Satisfactory/Unsatisfactory. At those colleges where independent study is compulsory, a completed project judged unsatisfactory must have its faults remedied or be replaced by a project of greater merit. Often if the work was done during a January intersession, the student must spend the following summer working on a new project.

Attempts at evaluating the use of independent study by respondents led to the following advantages offered for the use of independence:

1.   Students are encouraged to work independently and individual resourcefulness and self-discipline are fostered by the use of this approach.

2.   There is a closer interaction between faculty and students.

3.   Student-centered teaching is effective in improving problem solv-

ing and the ability to apply concepts to fresh situations and in promoting noncognitive changes.

Many respondents were in agreement that "generally students have approved the system."

As far as disadvantages are concerned, some colleges reported faculty reluctance or lack of enthusiasm for advising students on independent study, especially if the time and energy spent in this way were not deducted from the teacher's course load. Sidney L. Gulick, dean of arts and science at San Diego State College, California, for example, indicated that the disadvantage is "mainly more work for all concerned." He also stated, however, that "certainly to my mind the values gained far outweigh the disadvantages."

Concerning the drawbacks for students, a few respondents mentioned that some students complained of having had to work too hard on their independent study projects. Some administrators expressed concern over the readiness of all students to undertake independent study where such study is required. They felt that there are students who are unable to discipline themselves enough to work on their own. There were some who also stressed that the independent study approach cannot work successfully unless the instructor provides some preliminary structure. If such structure is not provided, "the student and the instructor could flounder the entire semester."

The president of St. Augustine's College, North Carolina, was one of the few respondents who indicated that there were high costs associated with independent study programs. It is reasonable to assume that where independent study is required, colleges must enlarge their libraries and increase the number of faculty members. Off-campus or foreign study programs require additional personnel to coordinate such efforts. All these factors result in increased costs to the college.[7]

One of the significant projects on independent study was directed by Sam Baskin at Antioch College in 1961. Titled "Experiment in Independent Study (1956–1960)," the report compared the learning achievement of two groups of academically comparable students, an experimental and a control group. Baskin's four-year experiment led him to conclude that students learned as much under the experimental method of independent study as under the traditional method of class work. He is not certain that independent study methods of instruction save instructional time, but he maintains that this is not the point. He ends the report by stating:

[7] Bonthius, Davis, Drushal, *et al., op.cit.,* pp. 193–210.

. . . The real promise of the studies is in the shift they may bring with them in the educational orientation of both students and teachers. Most important-ly, they argue for the far greater use of the student's own resources for learn-ing. They press us to shake ourselves loose from some of our educational habits, and they offer new assurances of the unused potential for learning—and one that we have hardly begun to tap—that exists within the student himself.

NON-WESTERN STUDIES

A rather significant development in the curriculum of liberal arts colleges relates to the need for all educated Americans to know more about other cultures and other peoples. During the present century the preoccupation of American higher education with domestic affairs has been dramatically reversed—gradually at first, but with growing momentum since World War II. The result has been a sharp reorientation of our academic out-look.

Five approaches can be identified as one examines the programs in colleges throughout the country. Some developments started earlier than others, and from time to time they have run together and influenced one another. These approaches are: (1) extracurricular fascination with the world overseas; (2) course work in international relations or world affairs; (3) general courses introductory to a civilization or a group of civiliza-tions; (4) infusion of non-Western material into regular disciplinary courses; (5) area studies as a formally recognized part of the curriculum.[8]

Since 1961 there has been an increase in the number of colleges of-fering systematic approaches to non-Western studies. (See Table 2.) More so than ever, faculties are concerned about curricular arrangements that will enable the majority of undergraduates to gain an understanding of the peoples of other lands, who now, because of increased communica-tions and rapid transportation, are really our neighbors.

[8] For a detailed report on non-Western Studies, see *Non-Western Studies in the Liberal Arts College,* A Report of the Commission on International Understanding (Washington, D.C.: Association of American Colleges, 1964). In addition to offer-ing the rationale of non-Western studies, and describing the origins and growth of non-Western studies, the report provides information and guidance for those col-leges that have not yet reached a decision, by presenting and analyzing experiences that have been accumulated. Detailed reports on individual programs are pre-sented. The programs include those at Earlham College, Florida Presbyterian College, Portland State College, The State University College at New Paltz, New York, Williams College, Hanover College, Marian College, Mills College, Western College for Women, California State College at Hayward, Occidental College, Dartmouth College, and the University of the Pacific, and also the cooperative pro-grams at Atlanta University Center, the Gettysburg Group, Great Lakes Colleges Association, the St. Paul Group, and the Winston-Salem Group.

Mills College, in California, which has been concerned since its founding with the study of Asia, several years ago began to increase the breadth and depth of Asian study offered its students. It has resulted thus far not only in an introduction of new materials in a variety of existing college courses but in an experimental course which holds promise of opening a wide area of complex material to nonspecialist study.

The need to increase Western knowledge of the rapidly developing non-Western areas of the world can hardly be overstated. The difficulty for a liberal arts college is in finding a means to provide, in the relatively short time available to undergraduates, a meaningful introduction to understanding both a complex traditional society and the forces and effects of its contemporary struggle to modernize.

Mills' first faculty seminar on non-Western studies was convened in 1961. Its leader was Harold H. Fisher, a noted historian and chairman emeritus of the Hoover Institute and Library at Stanford University, who came as a visiting professor to help Mills develop its non-Western program.

Fisher brought with him his conviction that, although a devoted specialization within a single academic discipline is the key to fruitful research, there is no reason to conclude that it is the key to the successful teaching of undergraduates. Thus he hoped to work out, with the help of specialists in many fields, a course which might be either supplementary or introductory to the discipline courses. Such a course would prepare some students for further study but, for many undergraduates, it could be their only formal intellectual contact with the living past and revolutionary present of the non-Western world.

Grants from the Asia Foundation and the Ford Foundation made possible the faculty seminars and the research assistance of Mrs. Rosemary Hornby, who became coauthor with Fisher of the syllabus. Members of the seminars were drawn from such seemingly foreign disciplines as mathematics, psychology, biology, and education, as well as from the arts, social sciences, and literature, in which there was already familiarity with some non-Western materials. Their study had two purposes: to provide orientation and education for the members so that new insights into non-Western cultures might be extended through the curriculum, and to bring the tools of all their disciplines to bear in developing the new course.

Styles of Civilizations, the course which evolved, is an educational experiment which attempts to comprehend the traditions of China and India in terms of their approaches to the basic problems common to all civilizations, and through this knowledge to seek understanding of the manner and means with which they are striving for modernization. In building the course, the second faculty seminar followed the same inter-disciplinary, problem-oriented route which is now presented to students.

Thus the study of, say, traditional Indian civilization began by asking how this civilization historically had attempted to solve the basic prob-lems—those of subsistence, social organization, and ideology. The stu-dents were not to be asked for a detailed description of a society's means of feeding and clothing itself, organizing power, or justifying itself in ideas. Rather they were to be asked to identify a manner or style of meeting these problems which is characteristic of the particular society, that is, to identify a distinctive manner of performing functions—economic or ritual, intellectual, aesthetic, or technical—which is recognizably Indian, or Chinese, or that of whatever society is studied. In recognizing a style, a student grasps the essential characteristics of a civilization. Here is the method, the heart, of the new course.

By the summer of 1964 a program had been created for this new kind of study of non-Western societies. It had taken form in a fifty-page syllabus, with over three hundred bibliographic entries chosen from thou-sands on China and India. "The 'Styles of Civilizations' course," ex-plains Edward LeFevour, course instructor,

may be described both as an effective introduction to non-Western studies, and as an innovating approach to interdisciplinary education. On either count it should be recognized as a singular achievement for a small liberal arts col-lege. That we are doing what other colleges hope to do and what universities hope to encourage is, in my view, a tribute to the innovating power of a liberal arts college.

Southern Illinois University recently began a program called Intercul, a program which is described by the dean of academic affairs as a small beginning for a large idea—that undergraduates at Southern Illinois have an opportunity to explore non-Western cultures in as great a depth as they desire and are able. To accomplish this the university has set up a director, a house, and informal opportunities for students to meet. The Intercul encourages innovative plans and new ideas for learning in non-Western fields, and offers students opportunities for extracurricular ac-tivities in non-Western activities or formal programs of study.

Another example of the growing trend is found in Amherst College in Massachusetts, which in cooperation with Mount Holyoke, Smith Col-lege, and the University of Massachusetts offers a program in Latin Amer-ican Studies in addition to offering its own special program in Asian and African Studies.

UNDERGRADUATE STUDY ABROAD

The growth of the number of programs which allow students to study abroad has been very rapid. In 1950 there were only six programs through which undergradautes could earn credit abroad during the academic year. Today, there are 598 institutions offering programs involving study abroad with over 50 per cent of this total introduced since 1961 and 63 other institutions planning to offer such a program in the near future. (See Table 2.)

Vassar College in New York and Bates College in Maine are representative of colleges which have well-established and very active Junior Year Abroad programs. At Vassar, qualified students may study abroad during all or part of the junior year with the approval of Vassar's Committee on Foreign Study. They receive leave of absence from Vassar, and are given academic credit on the satisfactory completion of their foreign program. The usual countries to which students go are England, France, Germany, Greece, Italy, Spain, and Switzerland. The major field of study is usually, although not always, the foreign language. In most of the programs there is an intensive study of language prior to the opening of the academic year. As a rule, students live as members of the family in private homes and take courses in a foreign university under the tutelage of that university's professors. There are variations of this pattern, however, which provide a certain amount of choice in the degree of guidance, supervision, and personal and academic freedom. Study abroad during the junior year is not limited to participation in only those programs listed; each year a few independent arrangements are approved by the Committee on Foreign Study. It should be realized, however, that no leave of absence can be granted nor Vassar credit given unless the student's plans have the approval of the Committee on Foreign Study.

To be favorably considered for Junior Year Abroad, a student must have personal and academic attributes that will enable her to gain significantly from foreign study, and to represent her program and Vassar College abroad. Her seriousness of purpose, adaptability, and intellectual and physical stamina must be such that she will be able to make a genuine contribution to whatever program she joins. Furthermore, she must have proved her ability to carry a Vassar course of study with better than average competence and responsibility. A cumulative average of about *B* is advisable for most programs, and an average of at least *B+* for study in Great Britain. A student generally offers at least two years of college work with a grade of *B* in the language of the country in which she wishes to study.

Early in the first semester of sophomore year, a student interested in Junior Year Abroad confers with the assistant to the dean of studies. This conference and subsequent ones with her major advisor and other departments concerned in her program are undertaken in preparation for a formal request to study abroad to be submitted to the Committee on Foreign Study. The committee meets early in February and, on the basis of academic records, recommendations from house fellows and professors, and the student's individual plans, makes its decision. If permission is granted, the student then applies to the Junior Year Abroad program she wishes to join. As a result of this selectivity, most candidates are accepted by the programs of their choice. Costs vary a good deal but, under most programs, are as high as the fees charged for a year at Vassar.

Bates College, Maine, normally enrolls about 10 per cent of the junior class in its Junior Year Abroad program. The Bates program differs from most of the others in that there is no organized program abroad, but instead the students are encouraged to apply as individuals to universities, chiefly in Britain and on the Continent, there to enroll and study just as would resident students. The program is available to any Bates junior, who stands decently well in his class and in his major field, and is elected by an especially high percentage of eligible women.

Under the name of Windham Abroad, Windham College in Vermont provides an enrichment of the educational offerings for its students by sponsoring programs of study and travel in Europe. Windham offers Summer Abroad programs where participating students travel in Europe for six weeks with instructors from the college. They visit historical sites during the day and have lectures and seminars in the evening. The college also offers the Semester Abroad such as the one in the fall of 1967 where a group of students went to France accompanied by two Windham College professors. The college engaged the use of the Chateau Charbonnières near Brou where the students and faculty lived and held classes. All costs for this program were covered by the regular semester fee, except personal expenses and independent travel during and after the semester. Windham also offers study-travel trips to Europe during the January intersession and during the summer session.

The programs that are offered are as varied as the institutions that administer them. They vary in time spent abroad, from the traditional academic year at one end of the spectrum to the summer program at the other, and in between are innumerable configurations. Some programs are restricted to students of the administering institution; others are open to students of all institutions. Phillips University in Oklahoma, for instance, does not restrict its annual European Study Tour to Phillips students. Originated in 1963 to provide students the opportunity to study and travel under the direction of a faculty member, the tour welcomes students from other institutions. Classes meet in the Louvre in Paris, in the Prado in Madrid, and in the Rijksmuseum in Amsterdam.

Programs also range widely in locale. Europe has been a favored site. In cooperation with the universities of Paris, Vienna, and Madrid, Central College in Iowa offers a twelve-month study program designed for students with good language competence and the self-discipline needed to attempt a rigorous university schedule. The program offers a maximum of 48 credits. For students of French, the program is offered in cooperation with the *Cours de Civilisation Française.* Summer courses focus on language and composition. In the fall and spring terms, students may elect courses in history, economics, political science, and humanities. For students of German, the program is offered at the Goethe Institute in the summer in Germany and in winter and spring at the University of Vienna. For students of Spanish, the program is offered at Santander and the University of Seville in the summer, and at the University of Madrid in the winter and spring.

More recently programs have been sprouting on other continents, first in Mexico, then elsewhere in Latin America, and now in Asia and Africa. While the College of Liberal Arts of the University of Arizona in Tucson has an annual Humanities Tour which visits Europe, they also have established a successful summer session in Guadalajara, Mexico. The program can handle between 650 and 700 students and the college takes over the complete facilities of a private school in Guadalajara during the summer months. The college employs a person in Guadalajara on a year-round basis whose sole responsibility is to locate those families from whom the students will gain most through residence in their homes during the summer session. The California State Colleges International Programs have established programs in cooperation not only with European universities but also with Waseda University in Tokyo and National University and National Chengchi University in Taiwan. In Lebanon, Princeton broke new ground by establishing the National Undergraduate Program for Overseas Study of Arabic. Wisconsin sponsors an Undergraduate Year in India and in Latin America. Columbia administers a summer anthropological program in cooperation with Cornell and Harvard Universities, and the University of Illinois.

OFF-CAMPUS STUDY IN THE UNITED STATES

Baker Brownell has criticized American colleges for permitting themselves to be the victims of what he has called "three corrupting principles." The substance of his criticism is that higher education is "still treated not as life but as a preparation for life," that the cloistered campus is unreal, and that the typical college does not relate theory to practice.[9] "If ways can be found," he writes, "whereby the student can have a significant part in events, he will respond maturely in most cases."[10]

Various ways are being tried by liberal arts colleges to involve students in off-campus experience as an integral part of their education.

WORK-STUDY PROGRAM

An increasing number of colleges are requiring work experience as a regular part of the student's college program. (See Table 2.) The concept of an off-campus work program is not a new one, but the last few years have witnessed a number of significant developments in cooperative plans. One such development is the adoption of calendar plans that require or encourage the student to spend one or more quarters of his college career in some kind of work activity or field or other off-campus project. New programs recently instituted at Kalamazoo College in Michigan, Earlham College in Indiana, and Beloit College in Wisconsin, are typical of these plans. The new Beloit plan, which went into effect in the fall of 1964, provides for a three-phase college calendar: (1) three trimesters on campus; (2) five trimesters—two on campus, one off campus, and two that may be used for vacation; and (3) a final three trimesters on campus. The off-campus term during the second phase may be used for independent study or research, or some other "real-world" experience in the United States or abroad, and both vacation terms may be used for this purpose.

Another pattern is that of cooperative education, particularly for the disadvantaged, a plan which integrates classroom instruction and work experience. The work experience constitutes a regular and essential element in the educative process, and a specified amount of time on the job and minimum standards of performance are included in the requirements for a degree. The cooperative job assignments are carefully planned and supervised to produce optimum educational results for each student.

The purpose of cooperative education is to add to the student's learn-

[9] Baker Brownell, *The College and the Community* (New York: Harper & Row, Publishers, Inc., 1952), pp. 35–38.

[10] Baker Brownell, "The Community in College Teaching," in R. Cooper, ed., *The Two Ends of the Log* (Minnesota: University of Minnesota Press, 1958), p. 284.

ing an element that is lacking in traditional programs: the work periods which help the student see relevances between classroom studies and the use of knowledge in the world of work. Students in cooperative plans also have the opportunity to sample possible careers in fields of their choosing. The purpose of the plan is distinctly educational, but an attractive by-product is that students can finance their education wholly or in part.

An illustration of the work-study approach for the disadvantaged student is the Cooperative Education Plan at Golden Gate College in California. Golden Gate undertook a three-year pilot project in the fall of 1965 to test the work-study program as a technique for developing the academic and vocational competence of youths who are economically deprived but have the necessary native ability. The project has been supported by a grant from the Fund for the Advancement of Education for salaries of special staff and other directly related expenses. All other costs, including those of testing, tutoring, and financial aid, have been met from other funds available to the college.

Summing up the progress report on the project, President Russell T. Sharpe stated:

It is too early to draw firm conclusions but we are encouraged to believe the work-study program is a realistic way of providing opportunities for economically disadvantaged youth to attend college, and concurrently gain creative work experience through part-time employment.

As a result of the study and of the decision by the National Commission on Cooperative Education to encourage more colleges to consider the adoption of cooperative programs, it is likely that new programs will be developed within the next few years and that these new programs will vary as widely as those in the past.

COMMUNITY SERVICE PROJECTS

Many colleges have long made use of community service projects as a major resource for student learning. Besides pioneering work at Antioch in Ohio, there were programs at Berea College in Kentucky and at Earlham College in Indiana. In 1947, for example, Earlham College inaugurated its Program of Community Dynamics, under which students help in community efforts at the request of community groups. Brooklyn College in New York City has had a community service program for a long time. Since 1948, the college has required that all education majors give two semesters of voluntary service in community agencies. A mimeographed statement from the Brooklyn College education department reports that a survey in 1957, which undertook to measure the effectiveness of the program, stated that "we may conclude that the improved preparation of our student teachers, with a wider insight into community as well as school problems and their solution, seems to result from the community participation program."[11]

More recently, the push is to involve students off campus in urban problems. In May 1963, the Associated Colleges of the Midwest and the Chicago Board of Education announced a Program in Urban Education, to begin in September 1963. The aim of the program was to provide advanced education students with special preparation for teaching in large urban centers. In 1965, Webster College in Missouri established Mullanphy House, better known as Chocolate House because of its rich brown color. Sponsored by the college, and an outgrowth of its social science department, Webster College's Chocolate House is situated in a deprived urban area and has established a preschool project as well as other educational and humanitarian programs. The House is under the supervision of Sister Therese Delich, an instructor in Webster College social science department; she is assisted by Sister Dennis Marie, a practical nurse, and several undergraduate Webster students from various departments.

The College of Arts and Sciences of Washington University in Missouri has, at the present time, two projects involving the local community. One is the Education in Action program under the auspices of the Student Activities Office. The program, which is especially interested in the "uncommitted Liberal Arts student," is designed to give students the opportunity to work in volunteer programs under supervision from the particular agency and the Education in Action staff. The other project is run by the Campus "Y" and is essentially a tutorial project for students in a nearly totally deprived community. Thus far the college has not given academic credit for either of these activities. In part, according to the dean of the college, "this is because of the fear of the directors of the projects that academic credit might be more harmful than useful to the projects."

In 1966 the student body and faculty of Allegheny College in Pennsylvania established the Allegheny Community Exchange (ACE) which has become the largest activity on campus, involving over 125 students. ACE volunteers participate in programs that bring them in contact with the Doman Cerebral Palsy Clinic, the Crawford County Juvenile Court and Probation Office, the Child Day-Care Center, including Project

[11]"The Contribution That Experience in Community Agencies Makes to the Professional Training of the Students in Our Teacher Education Program," Brooklyn College Education Department, New York, November 1959, part 2, p. 32. (Mimeographed.)

Headstart, adult and child tutorials, the YMCA, and the Boy Scouts. The Exchange's purpose is "to inspire a sense of social responsibility in the student and demonstrate to the townspeople that the campus community is aware of its obligation to a larger community than the college campus."

Adrian College and Siena Heights College in Michigan joined their tutorial programs during the spring of 1967 and provide students in teacher education with experience in working with children. The public and parochial schools of Adrian, Michigan, furnish the laboratory for the program while the college students give service to the schools voluntarily and gain experience from the program. Phillips University in Oklahoma and the Enid community complement each other in providing a better social, cultural, and intellectual environment for both the Phillips student and the Enid resident. One concrete example of mutual cooperation is the combined effort of the university and the community which gave birth to the Community Speech and Hearing Center on the Phillips campus. Phillips' appreciation of the historic background of the Enid area and its desire to preserve the colorful past of the early Cherokee Strip, combined with community support, produced the Cherokee Strip Museum.

Another approach to service is the program of Adult Education offered at West Georgia College; this is considered a distinct program of study, action, and community service. The 1964 Studycade to the World's Fair was one of the unique studycade experiences sponsored by the college through its adult education program. The group was made up of people representing a number of communities, different vocations, and various interests from the college community. There was a real desire on the part of all members of the group not only to enjoy traveling with each other but also to become knowledgeable about our country. West Georgia College Studycades have gone all over the United States, and studycaders have met new people, acquired knowledge and understanding of different cultural patterns, and exchanged ideas with people all over the country.

Those institutions that have adopted an off-campus plan as an integral part of their programs are convinced that they have great educational merit. Advantages described are that students seem to mature more rapidly; students develop a seriousness of purpose; students exhibit greater self-discipline, thereby improving their academic work; students see their campus studies in a broader context. Many colleges feel that off-campus study stimulates the entire campus. Students fresh from off-campus experience expect more of their teachers. They are readier to question and to dispute; they have experience to back them up. It is very clear that the boundaries of the campuses are expanding.

Chapter 3

NEW APPROACHES TO INSTRUCTIONAL METHODS

THE DEMANDS ON COLLEGE TEACHING IN THE 1970'S ARE VERY DIFFERENT from those of previous decades. Pressures of increasing enrollment, the explosion of knowledge, the fast pace of social change, and the availability of new technology combine to make the need for changes in college teaching imperative. Liberal arts colleges throughout the country are experimenting with instructional approaches in response to the demands on college teaching.

THE NEW MEDIA

The new media and technology have aroused more controversy than any other pedagogical development of recent years. At issue is how the new technology—televised instruction, computers, programmed courses, films, tapes, and other audio-visual materials—can be employed in teaching and learning, and whether these devices can be used to educate larger numbers of students without completely automating the educational process.

This is always a difficult tightrope to walk, for it is only too easy for us, in our desire to meet the problems of numbers and finances, to rationalize away all arguments about the importance of the dialogue between teacher and student as a significant component of the student's learning experience. Used in intelligent and sensitive balance, however, there is much that the new media can offer in our organization of higher education. Many colleges are using the products of technology as an integrated part of the instructional process in ways that extend the institution's instructional reach and provide individualized approaches to student learning.

TABLE 3 LIBERAL ARTS COLLEGES INVOLVED WITH INSTRUCTIONAL INNOVATIONS

Instructional Practice	Number of Usable Responses to Item [a]	Percentage of Usable Responses	Before 1961	Percentage of Responses	1961 and After	Percentage of Responses	Planning to Introduce	Percentage of Responses
Educational television	368	41.7	63	17.1	181	49.2	124	33.7
Teaching machines	224	25.4	37	16.5	147	65.6	40	17.9
Language laboratories	780	88.4	341	43.7	393	50.4	46	5.9
Programmed instruction	325	36.8	30	9.2	245	75.4	50	15.4
Interinstitutional cooperative programs	573	65.0	150	26.2	346	60.4	77	13.4
Dormitory as a learning center	200	22.7	41	20.5	77	38.5	82	41.0
Living-learning residence halls	115	13.0	36	31.3	50	43.5	29	25.2
Comprehensive examinations	474	53.7	310	65.4	131	27.6	33	7.0
Variations in grading practices	167	18.9	71	42.5	43	25.8	53	31.7
Team teaching	592	67.1	137	23.1	407	68.8	48	8.1
Teaching aides	521	59.1	252	48.4	241	46.2	28	5.4

[a] The total number of usable responses to the questionnaire was 882.

49

INSTRUCTIONAL TELEVISION

Several institutions are using closed-circuit television to bring outstanding lectures to very large numbers of students and then supplementing these lectures with small-group discussions. In 1966, for instance, West Virginia Wesleyan College was awarded a grant under the Federal program of providing educational materials to improve undergraduate instruction. As a result of this subsidy, the college constructed an on-campus television studio fully equipped to offer closed-circuit instructional services to the campus. Under this program repetitious lectures and demonstrations are planned on video tape, thus freeing the teacher to devote more time to students individually as well as providing an opportunity for more creative and challenging learning experiences. "All students have a front row seat regardless of class size," explains Walter L. Brown, assistant dean of the college, "which is important even in a small science class where students must have a magnified one-to-one student-instructor situation." The television studio has distribution lines to all parts of the campus allowing a free flow of information into every instructional area. The center at the University of Miami in Florida is another example. The university's facility is equipped to televise lectures by closed circuit to as many as 1,800 students at a time and to rerun these lectures on video tapes at any time. Key problems and issues growing out of the presentation are then taken up in small-group discussions. Similar programs are used at Pennsylvania State University, where, in addition, a specially devised telephone system enables students to ask the lecturer questions, even though they are hearing him in another lecture hall.

Television equipment owned by the College of Wooster in Ohio includes one Ampex 7000 VTR with monitor and a dolly-mounted GPL camera. Two additional VTR's of the same make, a Raytheon camera, and a ten-classroom closed-circuit television (CCTV) system are in the process of installation. During the past year the video tape system, described above, has been used for teacher and student criticism and performance evaluation in public speaking. On a few occasions it was used to augment or supplant lectures. With the new CCTV system, located in the main classroom building, extensive use is anticipated of taped programs from other institutions or from educational networks. In addition, plans at Wooster call for equipping a studio and ten classrooms for closed-circuit television presentations in the freshman liberal studies program. Through the use of CCTV it will be possible to have a lecturer present one lecture in the morning and then the tapes will be replayed to different sections of the same course throughout the day. Samuel Baskin, director of the Union for Research and Experimentation in Higher Education at Antioch College, Ohio, reports that Antioch has had extensive and good experience with a video tape facility. The video tape facility at Antioch consists of a seminar room equipped with four remote-control cameras. Instant playback is possible in the room. There are also three portable video recorders which can be used in a variety of settings and a kinescope machine with which to make film from edited tape. The setup is staffed by two full-time men with some part-time help provided by students.

The application of closed-circuit television on the Berkeley campus of the University of California is to support and encourage the face-to-face contact of teacher and student, and to introduce resources, experiences, and efficiencies not otherwise available to student-learning contexts including self-study, tutorial, seminar, discussion, laboratory, and lecture meeting formats. The majority of uses of television techniques by faculty and students involve the preparation and utilization of recorded presentations. Faculty and teaching departments representing all disciplines are accumulating an extensive library of recorded video tape and film presentations. Library recorded presentations follow, but are not limited to, three general forms of organization. Lectures average thirty minutes in length and are recorded as sequentially related direct-to-the-camera presentations and demonstrations. Modules are generally fifteen minutes or less in length, falling mainly in the life sciences, and are highly dependent and impersonalized presentations of processes or procedures. Documentaries are generally thirty minutes or longer and represent unique and unusual materials, interviews, or experiences. Where televised presentations from the video tape and film library are utilized as core instructional material, the average size of the viewing group ranges from twenty to thirty students in individual seminar, discussion, and laboratory sections conducted by the teaching staff. Opportunity for discussion prompted by the televised presentation and led by the instructor is regularly provided just prior to or just following the televised presentation.

The library of video tape and film at Berkeley is maintained at a Master Distribution Center (MDC). A closed-circuit wire television communication system is operated from the MDC. Production and technical support is provided to several satellite closed-circuit systems around the campus. Five buildings with a total of twenty-eight terminally equipped instructional spaces are connected to the MDC and are permanently equipped with television communication display stations consisting of a video monitor, a speaker amplifier, and accessory items. All terminal display stations serviced by the MDC are fully and remotely controlled from the MDC. From any room display station a voice request (via an intercommunication system) may be made at random to start, stop, or otherwise change a scheduled presentation. The MDC has now available to it five video tape sources, one 16mm film source, two VHF/UHF broadcast tuner sources, three live camera sources, and a variety of sound sources for individual or simultaneous distribution to one or more terminal room display stations in any combination. Production capability centers about a mobile video tape and television camera recording unit.

The program of television service covering the operation of all facilities, spaces, and schedule of production and distribution services outlined above, as well as administration of the television communication service program for the campus, is staffed by six full-time professional employees. Additional professional and student staff are employed on an hourly basis. Professional staff are exclusively involved in all planning, production, and technical aspects of video tape and film presentations. Professional technical staff additionally undertake and supervise the design, installation, operation, and maintenance of all television communication facilities in the Master Distribution system, as well as in the satellite television communication systems around the campus. Student staff, under supervision, operate the Master Distribution Center and "answer" calls for service from faculty and students from the terminally connected and equipped television communication display stations.

Educational television at Yale University is not used to solve classroom population problems, nor to record complete lectures for review or for posterity. It is used to collect exhibits teachers may wish to include in lectures, or to magnify, or to provide step-by-step instruction. In one instance, television cameras record the interactions of a small group of students and the recorded tape is the means by which these future sociologists learn to define group dynamics. According to David Walker, editor of *Yale Reports,* none of these uses constitutes an innovative practice when considered on technical grounds. However,

all are innovative for us because they are part of changing methods of teaching here. Each time a tape of an anatomy dissection is used by a teacher to illustrate a point produces a change of attitude on the part of the teacher. Each time an anatomy student replays the same tape he adds to or consolidates his knowledge. Each time a paleontologist observes how a 'possom's jaw muscles function with the aid of an image intensifier and videotape connected to his x-ray equipment knowledge is advanced too. In other words, the innovations I see here are educational, not technical.

Yale also has an audio-visual center which provides classroom services and centralized facilities for recording and editing. There is, in addition, the Yale–New Haven Educational Corporation which functions as a production agency.

The State University College at Buffalo, New York, is getting under way with a campus distribution system. In Rhode Island, Barrington College's use of educational television was initiated with the purchase of a video recorder in January 1968 for the purpose of recording classroom presentations of new course offerings of interdisciplinary studies. Television has been used in the Southern Colorado State College instructional program since 1964. The television center consists of a studio 40 feet square and a control room approximately 20 x 40 feet which houses two vidicon cameras, two Ampex VR 660 recorders, one Ampex VR 1000 recorder, a complete film projection chain, and the usual equipment for switching and special effects. Programs are produced either in the studio or on remote location by mobile van, then distributed on a prearranged schedule into viewing classrooms. A microwave link distributes programs between the Orman Campus and the Belmont Campus under construction across the city.

The Television Center with its professional staff, production and technical, operates as a service agency to the academic departments of the college. Instructors may schedule the use of the facility and receive expert consultation in the production of televised lectures, demonstrations, and other activities related to course objectives. The use of the medium as an evaluation or counseling device, as in micro-teaching or psychodrama, is encouraged. It is institutional policy to provide the student with a variety of learning resources which include television, book, film, tape, or other teaching aid. Television is integrated in the learning process to meet a particular need. In this sense, television becomes an accepted part of the classroom scene, whether it is for five minutes, twice during a quarter, or on a regular daily basis.

The common problem is existent at Southern Colorado State College to stimulate increased faculty interest and to overcome an inner threat that television might usurp the teaching role. To combat the problem, television equipment is made readily available to departments and faculty members, where needed, outside the Television Center facility. Opportunity is provided for faculty to become familiar with instructional television through informal experimentation as well as formally organized programming.

At Minot State College in North Dakota, the science division has implemented the teaching procedures employed in various courses by the use of television techniques. The use of television, in the opinion of the instructors involved, has been very useful and highly successful in some cases, while in other instances these techniques have been somewhat less than successful. The most successful use of television has been in courses designed to acquaint elementary school teachers with techniques of teaching science and in a course in physical science for secondary school teachers. Television techniques have also been used in connection with courses such as anatomy and physiology, where the instructor recorded certain details in the procedure used in the dissection of a dog. Television has been used by members of the science faculty to help cope with large enrollments. One additional anticipated use of television is in connection with Minot's astronomy course, where the faculty will use television to record special events such as eclipses. These can then be made available to the students for viewing as required. The science division plans to use television "more and more."

While many colleges are just beginning to get interested in the use of television as an instructional tool, colleges such as Stephens College in Missouri have been experimenting with closed-circuit television since 1955. The story of the original experiment which occasioned the installation and use of the closed-circuit system on the Stephens campus was centered on the innovation of a new course, Ideas and Living Today.[1] Over the years closed-circuit television on the Stephens campus has received widespread acceptance by faculty, students, and administration. The Ideas and Living Today course has proved invaluable as a means for providing students with a common experience under a free elective system. Students have benefited from opportunities for enrichment which would otherwise not have been available. Teachers have been encouraged to re-examine teaching methods for more effective presentation. Members of the faculty have become more aware of the interests and capabilities of colleagues who participate as lecturers on closed-circuit television. "We feel that the closed-circuit system," says Ralph Leyden, director of educational development at Stephens, "has helped us to improve the quality of our instruction."[2]

In contrast to the television facilities used from 1955 to 1962 are those now available in Stephens College in the new James Madison Wood Quadrangle. The new facilities, which incorporate many kinds of instructional services, are designed to meet educational needs as they might develop over the next fifty years. Concomitant with the use of closed-circuit

[1]For a complete history of the development and evaluation of the Ideas and Living Today course *see* Ralph C. Leyden, *10 Years of Closed Circuit TV at Stephens College, 1955–1965* (Missouri: Stephens College, January 1966). 115 pp.
[2]*Ibid.,* p. 91.

television in Ideas and Living Today, faculty in several departments experimented with the media's usefulness in other courses. At Stephens the hope is that television will not be looked upon merely as a device for extending the instruction by one individual. Leyden says,

Although this is an important consideration, especially when that individual is an exceptional teacher, there are other equally important reasons for using television. Faculties should be given time and resources to exploit the medium for making instruction itself as vivid and as effective as possible.[3]

Closed-circuit television has been in continuous use at Central Connecticut State College since 1958. Kansas State College of Pittsburgh played a pioneering role in the development of closed-circuit television as a teaching tool. Pilot studies made at Kansas State as early as 1956 aimed at determining the effectiveness of this new medium. San Francisco State College was an early starter with its first on-campus instructional television presentation started in the spring semester of 1963.

Not all developments in television pedagogy are concerned with direct instruction. One exciting trend in colleges involved in teacher training is the growing use of video tape playbacks of live class meetings. Abilene Christian College in Texas operates a "Campus School," grades 1–12, which is used for observation and student teaching in the Teacher Education Program. Each room in the building is wired for television, both audio and video. Cameras are attached to the walls at the front and at the rear of the room, and remotely controlled by the instructor of the college class in professional education in the classroom building. As this instructor, for example, in teaching arithmetic, wishes her students to observe the pupils and teacher in fifth-grade arithmetic, she may do so by pressing a button. At St. Cloud State College in Minnesota, closed-circuit television is employed by the campus laboratory school in several ways. Taped recordings of individual classes are made and played back for students in educational courses. This is especially helpful in providing a live experience for the students to observe and in providing a basis for discussing the teaching-learning process. Another use made of the taped recordings relates to inservice training of the staff. A review of teaching a particular class provides valuable information to the regular teacher in two ways. First, it is the basis for self-improvement, and second, it provides the setting for experimentation with new methods and materials. At the present time the campus school is researching various procedures and techniques such as micro-teaching, modular scheduling, programmed instruction, and the use of teaching machines. Indiana Central College has developed

[3] *Ibid.*, pp. 113–114.

a "micro teaching program" for their student teachers during the semester in which they do all their work within the department of education and the classroom to which they are assigned for student teaching. This micro-teaching program is set up by bringing students from the public schools into classrooms at Indiana Central. A student teacher presents a unit of material, and her procedure is put on tape. After her student-teaching colleagues and the students have evaluated her presentation, the tape is available so that she can see herself in a teaching situation. Central Washington State College uses closed-circuit television in the same manner as Indiana Central.

The faculty of Hunter College, New York, regarded the installation of a closed-circuit television system in 1959 as more than a new audio-visual aid with a potential of teaching students en masse. The new medium was installed after considering possibilities for improving the observation process in the Hunter College Campus Schools and for facilitating research in important areas of teacher education. Hunter College places approximately 1,000 student teachers each year, most of them in school systems in the metropolitan New York area and a few in the two College Campus Schools. The many demands of a strong liberal education at Hunter College leave room for only a half-day's student teaching for one semester. Faculty and students alike are convinced that any respectable program of teacher education must depend to a great extent on the actual school classroom situation. However, the sheer physical requirements of the growing teacher education programs limit the possibility of the classroom continuing to serve effectively for demonstration, observation, and practice. Increasing attention is being given at Hunter to ways in which live and recorded closed-circuit television may maintain and enhance use of the classroom as a vital practice resource. Hunter College is exploring ways in which closed-circuit television might secure the following benefits: (1) observation of elementary school classes without admitting to the classroom any adult but the teacher, (2) recording of class activities in order to resolve problems arising from the difficulty of coordinating children's schedules with college calendars, (3) recording of student-teaching performance so that teaching candidates may see themselves in action, and (4) improvement of research on teaching where it is necessary to record teacher and student behavior.

In 1959, a closed-circuit television system was installed which connects seven originating rooms in the elementary school housed in one wing of the Hunter College skyscraper structure, three receiving rooms in a wing housing the education department, and a control room in the corridor connecting these wings. The originating rooms were equipped to enable transmission to college classes without changing the fundamental nature of the teaching-learning situation in the classes being observed. Accordingly, no operator is present in the room at the time of televising, but a remote-control system operates equipment in all ways. Rooms were not set up as studios but retained their character as elementary school rooms with normal-sized classes.

Research with television at Hunter developed a conviction that the new medium can make a significant contribution to educational inquiry. In addition, the student teachers' subjective reaction to use of the new medium was generally favorable. This response arose primarily from student teachers' feelings that they were being helped, were learning, and were getting not only special attention but an experience not otherwise available. The Hunter College Television Center has not chosen to engage in the usual closed-circuit applications of providing direct instruction of entire courses or parts of courses via the medium. However, the installation required for direct instruction can, without any or at most with minimal adaptation, fulfill this function as well.[4]

Other colleges have reported their evaluations of the use of educational television. St. Francis College in Indiana indicated that they found certain advantages in the use of television as a teaching tool. They include economy, visualization of concepts and processes which often require tremendous duplication of effort to be presented in other ways, and finally "as a self-evaluation tool video tape is unparalleled." St. Francis also reported good student reaction. Disadvantages include the increased work load on the television teachers and equipment reliability. However, the audio-visual director of St. Francis College feels that these disadvantages can be remedied. The associate dean of the College of Arts and Sciences of Loyola University in Chicago reports that at the present time the use of educational television facilities is declining. "I feel that we have not used them properly," he says, "but at the same time I do know that it is difficult to persuade faculty members that TV can be of help to them." The director of program development and research at Loretto Heights College in Colorado indicates that "at present we have equipment for TV instruction, but it is not in use. The equipment was strangely gotten through a grant with no one to operate it!"

The College of Liberal Arts of the University of Arizona has conducted studies of comparative achievement of students in a television course and students in sections of the same course taught in the more traditional manner. On the basis of that particular criterion the dean of

[4]Statements by Herbert Schueler, director of teacher education, and Milton J. Gold, professor of education.

the college reports that the results have been pretty much the same following both methods of presentation.

We have learned from experience that the instructor has to appreciate the fact that instruction on television requires special personal characteristics, special techniques and an unusual amount of preparation, and a new television instructor must be willing to work with and seek the advice of seasoned performers.

TEACHING MACHINES

A number of institutions are conducting experiments in the use of computer technology in instruction. I.B.M. is developing a program known as Computer Assisted Instruction which permits sending programmed courses by telephone wire to any location in the country. Thus, a student sitting at a computer typewriter station anywhere in the United States can hook into and receive immediate feedback on a computer-programmed course originated in the I.B.M. Research Center at Yorktown Heights, New York. Several universities, including Pennsylvania State, Florida State, and the University of Michigan are currently tied into the I.B.M. program. Still other developments in computer-assisted instruction can be illustrated by the Project Plato Program at the University of Illinois. Project Plato uses a computer-controlled system of slides, television displays, and student response panels for teaching a number of students simultaneously while still allowing each student to proceed at his own pace. In the program being developed at Pitzer College in California, freshmen take at least one programmed course, using computer consoles located in the residence hall.

On January 30, 1966, Oklahoma Christian College went into full operation with one of the largest dial access systems being used in instruction today. Each student is provided with his own permanently assigned learning carrel. Oklahoma Christian has 1,016 such carrels and assign them by the trimester. This carrel becomes the hub of the student's academic program, providing him with a study center of his own in an environment conducive to study. From it he may go to class or to the library or to a laboratory, but after a period in some other activity he will return to his carrel for the work which he does individually. The carrel is located in the same building with the library so that he has easy access to library resources. From his carrel he may dial any one of 136 tape-recorded sources available to him simultaneously. A weekly directory indicates that some of these sources will be played on a scheduled basis so that by choosing one of the perhaps twenty times during the week it will be played, he may access it at the same time others do but hear it from the beginning without interruption. Other materials, which are in less demand, are left to be started by dialing. These materials are available at any time a student might wish to use them. Teachers request the materials which they wish to make available each week. In addition, the student may check out an 8mm loop film projector, a slide or filmstrip projector, or a recorder to use in his carrel. The dean of instruction reported that a three-semester study of Oklahoma Christian College's Learning Center indicates that

students spend an average of fifteen hours a week in their carrels, that they have checked out 40 per cent more two-week library books than they did prior to the Learning Center, that they are studying about 25 per cent more hours per week than they did previously, and that the response to their carrels is favorable.

The Grand Valley State College dial access integrated audio-video system employs 256 carrels housed in the library area of Lake Superior Hall, one of the academic buildings. One hundred and thirty-one of these carrels are equipped for reception of closed- and open-circuit television, using monitors checked out at the library desk. One hundred and seven carrels have dial access to 120 audio program sources; 24 of these also function as a language laboratory, receiving a direct feed from a remotely located teacher console and providing remote record capability. Another group of 24 carrels, serving as a second language laboratory, receives audio programs from a second teacher console. Both consoles feed programs either by dialing from the audio system or by playing tapes and cartridges manually. The remaining carrels will be equipped as the need arises.

The audio distribution system employs twenty-four reel-to-reel type cartridge playback units and six reel-to-reel decks all equipped with four quarter-track playback heads for a total of 120 audio program sources. Any number of students can dial into the same program at the same time.

Twenty-four cartridge record-reproduce units serve as remote slave machines. These record the master tape and the student's voice. By dialing, the student can fast forward, play, or rewind this tape.

Dial access to audio programming is also available in classrooms and lecture halls on the campus, providing faculty with access to the materials. Dial accessing of the 120 program sources is accomplished by crossbar switching gear.

Eight television channels are available for distribution of live, video taped, filmed, or off-air programming to carrels, classrooms, and lecture halls. A film chain, two helical scan video tape recorders, and live cameras provide most of the video feeds.

Selected lectures are remotely recorded in the control room for use on the audio-visual system. Audio materials in language, primarily, but also in such diverse areas as music, mathematics, chemistry, and art, have been recorded in the audio studios for presentation on the dial system. Materials from outside sources, such as prerecorded language tapes, are often used.

Professional recording and duplicating equipment is used to achieve fine-quality audio masters for use on the audio-visual system. Television facilities include a studio equipped with five vidicon cameras, two studio control consoles (one designed for portability), and two helical scan VTR's. Professional graphic art support rounds out the television production facilities.

Some classrooms and lecture halls are wired for video transmission and can serve as studios if necessary.

Video taped productions are made at the request of individual professors or departments. These include single supplementary programs or integral segments of courses.

All academic departments use the dial access audio system to present materials ranging from supplementary to total teaching. The language department, in addition to its two language laboratories, is the heaviest user of the dial system.

West Virginia Wesleyan College in Buckhannon has a newly installed dial access retrieval system. This allows any student to dial directly into an information bank from any Centrex telephone on campus. Specifically, a student can pick up his dormitory telephone and retrieve instructional information scheduled by his professor. Instructors at Wesleyan are programming for retrieval such information as: how to prepare effective term papers; how to pronounce difficult science terminology; how to review effectively for a forthcoming examination.

Early in the fall of 1968 Beloit College in Wisconsin introduced a computer remote access terminal system. Beloit intends in the future to use computer-assigned instruction (CAI) and information retrieval.

The increasing enrollments in colleges and universities in New York State, combined with the shortage of outstanding instructors, has led the State University of New York at Albany to develop a comprehensive plan for the use of new media. Albany has participated in a state-wide CAI network using programs that are available from I.B.M. Recently, another aid, called the Student Response System (SRS), has been installed. The new Student Response System furnished by the General Electric Company, having the capability of nonlock and lock-step recording and computer analysis, opens up new areas of research directed at improving large-class instruction as well as proving the merit of a student response system. Similar student response systems are already in operation at Syracuse University in New York and Southern Illinois University.

While the future of teaching machines is bright indeed, liberal arts colleges are still a few years away from a meaningful use of computers and other teaching machines for instruction. Michigan State University uses television and programmed instruction but teaching machines are not used on campus for direct instruction. Where they have been used, it has been to develop and test materials which eventually find their way into a printed text version. This is the only advantage they have found in the use of teaching machines. The faculty have found many disadvantages such as (1) cost of purchase and maintenance, (2) supervision required for students, (3) cost of reproduction of materials into a machine format, and (4) general student dissatisfaction with the mechanics of the process. Weimar K. Hicks, president of Kalamazoo College in Michigan, reflects many of the liberal arts colleges when he says "looking ahead, we can see that in a few years these things will become common items in our classrooms. Right now, we are using a 'low key' approach to the problem."

LANGUAGE LABORATORIES

Language laboratories are now installed in most colleges around the country. (See Table 3.) In spite of the fact that much research is needed to learn what formats, patterns, drills, and the like are most effective, sufficient evidence has been gathered to show the practical values of the language laboratory.[5] There is great variety in the types of equipment that have been designed to serve language learning requirements. These include simple recorders; systems that permit the student to listen and then record his own response, which he can compare with the master tape; telephone dialing systems for tapes; combinations of tapes, printed materials, still pictures, or films; and finally, a wireless language laboratory in which each student wears a headset containing a small transistorized receiver that receives its audio signal from an antenna in the classroom. Thus, the need for wiring is obviated, and any classroom can become a language laboratory.

[5] For studies and developments in this area, see Gustave Mathieu, "Language Laboratories," *Review of Educational Research*, 32:2, 168–178, American Educational Research Association, Washington, D.C., April 1962; A. A. Lumsdaine, "Instruments and Media of Instruction," in N. L. Gage, ed., *Handbook of Research on Teaching: A Project of the American Educational Research Association* (Chicago: Rand McNally & Company, 1963); and F. R. Morton, *Recent Developments in Language Laboratory Equipment for Teaching and Research*, Language Laboratory Publication 5 (Ann Arbor, Michigan: University of Michigan, 1961).

PROGRAMMED INSTRUCTION

In technical terminology, programmed instruction is a teaching instrument whose task is to shape or change behavior toward specific goals. This change in behavior is called learning. In practical terms, programmed instruction is a method of teaching without the teacher's presence. Essentially, it is a systematic approach to self-instruction.

Programmed instruction has four special characteristics. The first characteristic is active responding. A second characteristic is immediate confirmation whereby a student sees directly after making a response whether it is correct. Correct responses enhance learning. A third characteristic of programmed instruction is steps that are small enough to let a student work through a program with a minimum number of errors. These small steps are carefully sequenced to lead from material that is familiar into and through material that has to be learned. A fourth characteristic is that the student proceeds at his own pace—another factor that aids learning.

Programmed instruction is used at colleges to provide for three distinct needs: remedial, supplementary, and enrichment. Programmed learning achieves a more effective and efficient approach to instruction by combining the careful analysis of the tasks to be learned, specification of the performance expected of students, and a thoroughly tested teaching strategy. The final version of a program is the product of applied learning principles and revisions resulting from student tryouts.

California State College at Hayward operates a Center for Independent Study (CIS) which utilizes programmed instructional materials in the form of textbooks and teaching machines. CIS has a part-time coordinator and is staffed by four part-time teaching assistants and four part-time student assistants. This complex, in its fourth year of operation, serves approximately 12 per cent of the student enrollment annually. Faculty members take advantage of the learning opportunities afforded their students at CIS by making assignments that must be completed at the center. The dean of instruction at the college feels that the gain to the instructor is such that he can devote more classroom time to lectures, covering topics in more depth or topics that he would normally not cover. Pre- and posttests, attendance, and allied reports are submitted to the instructor by CIS staff personnel. Students use CIS for a variety of reasons: to become familiar with material that is not normally offered in the college curriculum, to prepare themselves for entry into courses for which they have inadequate qualifications, or as an aid in keeping up in a class where their performance is below standard.

The primary reasons for the success of CIS, according to the dean, is the programmed, self-instructional materials that make up the bulk of the resources. These materials, carefully selected, permit students to work independently and achieve success. Most of the programs are in textbook form rather than on teaching machines, as they find they are more reasonably priced and easier for students to use in the center's present facilities.

From 1962 to 1965 the College of Wooster in Ohio participated with eleven other members of the Great Lakes Colleges Association (GLCA) in a three-year project to determine the feasibility of utilizing programmed materials in small liberal arts colleges and universities.[6] Approximately ten Wooster faculty members participated in a significant way in the project. Some of them field-tested commercially produced programs, while others tested programmed materials produced by faculty members within the GLCA. Professor Budd Russell of the physics department reported that students responded favorably to the material and achievement was as high as with the traditional textbook approach. The mathematics department, which in the fall semester of 1964 experimented with a large class of 100 students using the TEMAC program "Analytic Trigonometry," reported that the experimental group using the program achieved on the tests as well as the groups using only lectures. However, student attitudes toward the program were rather negative. In the economics department, a programmed text entitled *Micro Economics* was used approximately one-third of the semester to supplement the regular textbook in a beginning course in Principles of Economics. The text was acceptable to a majority of the students but the chairman of the department reported that the top-ability students found it boring and unimaginative.

The faculty of the College of Wooster are experimentally minded and particularly interested in new teaching techniques. Programmed materials have been used in all three of the major divisions of the curriculum —the natural sciences, the social sciences, and the humanities. In general, the most profitable use of programmed materials at Wooster has been as a supplement to other teaching methods, and not as a replacement for another form of presentation. The College of Wooster intends to continue to use programmed instruction.

The Programmed Learning Laboratory (PLL) was instituted at Bennett College, North Carolina, in 1965. Perhaps the most dramatically suc-

[6] For a complete description of the project see the final report which is available from the Bureau of Research, Office of Education, U.S. Department of Health, Education and Welfare, under the title "The Use and Development of Programmed Materials and Media in Private Liberal Arts Colleges," Project No. 5–0988 (B365), June 1966.

cessful use of the PLL has been in the classes of Mrs. Virginia Tucker, chairman of the school's Freshman English core program. Mrs. Tucker has used the laboratory for three years and is very enthusiastic about the use of programmed instruction.

Norman Licht, director of the Programmed Learning Laboratory at Bennett College, reports many advantages of the program. As far as advantages for students, the program is one means of motivating the student to perform. Programmed instruction allows students to learn at their own pace, permitting some to move through the materials quickly and others to spend additional time acquiring the necessary skills. The pretests and posttests provide the students with knowledge of how well they are performing. The student gets the benefit of more individual attention since the instructor is not used as a source of information, but rather as an advisor. The students are learning independent work habits by keeping their own test records and using the teacher as a resource to attain specific objectives. As for faculty members, Licht indicates that the instructors involved in the program are learning that they can be more effective when interacting with students:

When properly oriented to programmed instruction, an instructor discovers the power of this instructional strategy. Some faculty members have thought that programming dehumanizes learning through automating techniques. However, they soon learn that the instructor is the major factor which will determine whether the program will succeed or fail.

LEARNING RESOURCE CENTERS

Within the past decade the total amount of information available to serve the needs of mankind has nearly doubled. By 1980 it will have more than doubled again. In an era of space satellites and instant worldwide communications, traditional methods of gathering and transmitting information are no longer adequate to satisfy man's insatiable desire and incessant need for knowledge. Recognizing the importance of planning today for the needs of future generations of students, liberal arts colleges around the country have constructed a dramatic new concept in educational facilities—the college learning resources center.

What is a learning resource center, and how does it differ from a traditional college library? Unlike the more conventional library, which contributes to the broadening of knowledge through the written word in the form of manuscripts, books, newspapers, and periodicals, the modern learning resource center supplements and reinforces the impact of those important documents by providing for the storage and transmission of knowledge in audio and visual forms such as tape recordings, records, photographs, slides, motion pictures, and television. Thus the learning resource center introduces an important new dimension into the educational process by activating more of the senses. By involving the audio sense, as well as the visual, the important elements of emotion, involvement, and motivation have been heightened in the educational experience.

At the same time, the learning resource center introduces action to learning. This is a place where people do things; where learning is dynamic and involved, rather than passive and restrained. It is a place where students and teachers try new ideas; where learning is a shared experience; where the best of tradition comes to life and is made more meaningful; and where experimentation and innovation are the rule, rather than the exception.

The Elmira College Library/Learning Resources Center is being developed to incorporate the most recent developments in audio-visual and electronic media resources, in addition to a substantially increased number of books. The 75,000-square-foot structure is scheduled for completion in July of 1969. One of the significant features of the center will be approximately 400 carrels or individual study areas for students and faculty. Added to the private study areas in the residence hall and elsewhere on campus, there will be individual study spaces available for about 800 of the undergraduate student population of 1,400 anticipated by 1970. The carrels will be wired to accept dial access information retrieval equipment and closed-circuit television.

The State University of New York College at Cortland has a new (1967) learning resource center on its campus, as do many of the SUNY colleges. Florida Atlantic University was planned with learning resources as a core for the institution. A learning resource center has been established at Fairmont State College in West Virginia. The center occupies the first floor of the Fairmont State College Library and includes a multimedia presentation laboratory with tele-lecture facilities, a preview room, a graphics studio, equipment storage and repair laboratory, the director's studio, and a central office. Services planned include consultation with faculty and students to develop, produce, and present multimedia instruction. In addition the center will design and produce overhead transparencies, film slides and filmstrips, and audio tapes. Motion picture films and other media will be distributed on reservation by faculty and students. An equipment maintenance and repair facility will be responsible for keeping all audio-visual devices in proper running condition.

Future plans call for the development of a demonstration classroom center, campus-wide distribution of closed-circuit television through an information retrieval system, computerized instruction, and service to the public schools of Marion and surrounding counties.

Learning resource centers are being planned and established to help solve the logistical, strategic, and tactical problems involved in making available whatever instructional means and materials are needed to accomplish the instructional goals. The learning resource centers include and emphasize library materials, but in addition they include all other new media that are appropriate to the instructional functions of colleges and universities. Generally it is planned that these centers would not only procure but also produce instructional materials to specifications. Current thinking about learning resource centers tends to emphasize new media like films of all kinds, audio and video tapes, graphics, models, simulation mechanisms, and programmed instruction. The emphasis is on achieving enough flexibility to make instructional materials available to students when and where desired.

The Office of Instructional Resources of the University of Illinois at Chicago Circle supports instruction in Chicago Circle courses by providing media services and planning assistance. It is primarily concerned with the improvement of instruction, although, because of particular personnel capability and facilities, it also supports the conduct and presentation of research projects and fulfills administrative requirements. The Office of Instructional Resources (OIR) is organized into four principal divisions: programmed instruction, course development, television, and audio-visual, plus one auxiliary service, the Graphic Design Service.

INTERINSTITUTIONAL COOPERATIVE PROGRAMS

Interinstitutional cooperation may be defined as the voluntary collaboration between two or more institutions of higher education for the purpose of increasing the range and improving the quality of their services. It is a device enabling institutions to do better cooperatively what one or more of them may already be doing separately. In some instances, it enables institutions to do what neither of them could do separately.

Because of the accelerating growth of new knowledge it is all but impossible for even the largest institution to be all things to all men; however, division of labor and specialization enables institutions to provide a much wider range of services. The proponents of cooperation maintain, therefore, that more cooperative experiments are needed in order to provide quality education and other cultural services demanded by society. Other advantages articulated by those involved in cooperation are the help offered in experimenting as well as the economies that can be made. The small institution, especially, stands to gain from the economies of size and from access to faculty and facilities normally beyond its reach.

Cooperation may take many different forms. Cooperation can be regional, such as the New England Board of Higher Education (NEBHE) which serves the six New England states; the Southern Regional Education Board (SREB) which joins sixteen Southern states; and the Western Interstate Commission for Higher Education (WICHE) which serves thirteen Western states, including Alaska and Hawaii. Each of these organizations has a governing board or commission made up of persons appointed by the governors of the member states. It must be remembered, however, that the regional agencies are organizations of states, not of institutions, and thus differ from the other cooperative arrangements to be described.

Cooperation may take the form of multilateral arrangements with a minimum of organizational structure. For example, Judson College in Illinois is a charter member of the Associated Colleges of the Chicago Area (ACCA), a consortium of colleges organized for the purpose of interinstitutional cooperation. At the present time, arrangements are largely in the area of programs in science. The most significant of these has involved cooperation between ACCA colleges and Argonne National Laboratories, a project which has provided personnel and equipment which none of the cooperating colleges is able to afford individually. Guilford College, Bennett College, and Greensboro College, in North Carolina, have joined in a cooperative program which provides for interchange of students and library resources, and the possibility of a joint program in teacher education.

In 1965 ten experimental colleges, from New England to Missouri, formed the Union for Research and Experimentation in Higher Education (UREHE), a cooperative venture to study ways of improving teaching and learning. Member colleges are Antioch in Ohio, Bard in New York, Chicago Teachers College North in Illinois, Goddard in Vermont, Monteith College in Michigan, Nasson in Maine, New College of Hofstra University in New York, Sarah Lawrence in New York, Shimer in Illinois, and Stephens in Missouri. Two years later, New College in Florida and Loretto Heights in Colorado were added to the Union. The Union, with headquarters at Antioch College, is a consortium of colleges which have joined to encourage research and innovation in higher education. One of the programs is "project change-over," which will enable sixty college teachers to design and test new practices over a three-year period. Samuel Baskin, Union president, and director of the office of program development and research at Antioch College, indicated that innovation might include new teaching patterns to foster independent study, and reorganization of courses to cut across departmental boundaries and decrease proliferation.

Other cooperative groups that have developed are what Bunnell and Johnson call the larger corporate groups for cooperation.[7] In 1961, for instance, the Great Lakes Colleges Association was organized including Albion, Antioch, Denison, DePauw, Earlham, Hope, Kalamazoo, Kenyon, Oberlin, Ohio Wesleyan, Wabash, and Wooster. Another corporate group is the College Center of the Finger Lakes, an aggregation of seven small colleges in south and central New York State, also founded in 1961.

The Dormitory as a Learning Center

A recognition that to a growing extent the lives of undergraduates are being unhappily divided into two separate and unrelated experiences—the academic world of classroom, laboratory, and library, in contrast to the social world of the residence hall or other living arrangements on the periphery of the campus—has led several colleges to rethink the place of the dormitory on college campuses. A growing sense of alienation on college campuses, a growing awareness that learning can take place not only in college classrooms but anywhere and everywhere, recognition that the student spends more time in his dormitory than in classrooms—all these concepts have led a growing number of colleges to attempt a more meaningful use of residence facilities. (See Table 3.)

The pilot Program of the College of Literature, Science, and the Arts of the University of Michigan is an example of attempts to attack impersonality and academic isolation in a large college through the use of residence halls. In the spring of 1962 the dean and the Executive Committee of the College of Literature, Science, and the Arts of the University of Michigan opened discussion on ways to counter undesirable consequences of rapid growth at the university. The Executive Committee members were of the opinion that Michigan—like every major, expanding university—was suffering under the curse of impersonality. It was recognized that these not unrelated ills of growth and anonymity bear most heavily on underclassmen, especially freshmen. Fortunately, since all freshmen and many sophomores lived in university residence halls, it seemed feasible to develop a plan to integrate living and study among underclassmen. And if such a plan could place students in small-group units where instructors, advisors, and fellow students could become acquainted, possibly the specter of impersonality could be dispelled.

[7] Kevin P. Bunnell and Eldon L. Johnson, "Interinstitutional Cooperation," in Samuel Baskin, editor, *Higher Education: Some Newer Developments* (New York: McGraw-Hill Book Company, Inc., 1965), p. 259.

To these ends, the Executive Committee brought the Pilot Program into being in the fall of 1962 and specified the following provisions for implementation. First, certain sections of ten courses frequently elected by freshmen were reserved for members of one men's house and one women's house. Second, resident advisors (graduate students of high academic achievement) were placed in these two houses and were accorded the status, salary, and other perquisites of teaching fellows. Third, responsibility for the program was lodged in an *ad hoc* committee composed of four members of the college faculty and three representatives of the university residence halls. The budget for the project was provided by Vice-President Heyns from special funds. Its staff, apart from resident fellows, consisted of one graduate student who functioned as its coordinator.

From 1962 until 1965 the program followed essentially the same pattern. The number of participating student houses increased to four, and the roster of courses in which pilot sections were reserved increased in proportion. Continuing assessments, some formal, others not, were undertaken during these years to gauge the merit of the program. All the surveys indicated that pilot students respond favorably to the program, but this is hardly surprising since each student enters it as an informed volunteer. The most thorough and latest of the surveys showed that in contrast to a control group of 200 randomly selected college freshmen, pilot freshmen expressed satisfaction with residence hall life in general, and a significant proportion of them plan to remain in their halls after the freshman year. How much the program is affecting the intellectual bent of its students is less clear. To illustrate, in the winter term of 1966, two of the three male pilot houses placed third and fourth in grade-point averages for men's residence halls—first and second place fell to the two honors houses—but in the preceding term one of these pilot houses had placed below the men's average. It is perhaps too early to see any clear pattern emerging. Moreover, it is doubtful that objective standards can ever measure the kind of intellectual change the program hopes to effect.

By early 1966 the program was continued on a more stable basis and the annual budget administered from and by the College of Literature, Science and the Arts.

What is the rationale for a program such as the Pilot Program of Michigan? Perhaps more than ever before freshmen arrive at college campuses ready to learn in the fullest sense. Perhaps also more than ever before, today's undergraduate is markedly influenced by the views of his generation, by the goals, standards, tastes, interests, and values of fellow students. Thus, his experiences outside the classroom, on the fringe of the academic world, become powerful agents of change. Although the colleges of the country have sought—some aggressively—to reach students' minds in the classroom, they have rarely entered the social world of students other than in a mildly regulatory role. Those involved in the Pilot Program indicate that the program would make the means to a rationally unified campus life available to the student in the residence hall, "encouraging, but not forcing, the interpenetration of academic and social experience."

In volunteering to live in a pilot house and to enroll in one or more pilot sections, the student enters into the following specific elements of the program:

1. He finds himself in classrooms with acquaintances from his residence hall, and ideally a part of this shared intellectual experience is carried back and continued in the hall. Most instructors of pilot sections report that those classes are more responsive than nonpilot classes.

2. In his residence hall the pilot student associates with resident fellows who are graduate students selected expressly to function not only as resident advisors but also as somewhat older exemplars of a serious commitment to the academic life. Although they are not expected to act as tutors or professional counselors, the "RF's" do assist students, when approached, with academic problems and personal difficulties. Staffing pilot houses with these able and recent veterans of undergraduate education has undoubtedly been the critical element in the success of the program.

3. The pilot student has a chance to become acquainted with faculty members under relaxed social circumstances.

Ripon College in Wisconsin represents an approach that many liberal arts colleges are taking in attempting to use the residence halls as instructional centers. In November 1966, the Committee on Experimental Programs, composed of students, faculty, and administrators, proposed the establishment of a residential and instructional center at Scott Hall on the Ripon Campus. The program brought together a group of students with diversified backgrounds and abilities but with a common educational experience. The educational experience included enrollment in a history course, English course, and fine arts course. In addition to meeting in class, residential seminars were conducted in the residence hall. An evaluation of the residential seminars showed that the programs were judged to be satisfactory by all participants. A preliminary review of the grades led to few secure conclusions. The one test administered in an attempt to determine extracurricular learning did indicate that the experimental group ranked higher in tests for ability to integrate knowledge.

In order to facilitate the academic process and make for a more enlightened and productive student body, the seven residence halls at Kentucky State include academic, cultural, athletic, recreational, and social programs. The committee in charge of the academic program starts with the premise that life in a residence hall should be a learning experience and the first real task of the committee is the establishment and maintenance of an atmosphere where effective study can be pursued. A program of student self-help or tutorials, area study groups proctored by volunteers, and the designation of study areas with a basic reference library easily available are some of the activities provided in residence halls.

Many of the colleges reporting that they used the dormitory as a learning center merely provided study halls reserved for student use. Others stated that dormitories are considered learning centers in the sense that they not only house students but also members of the faculty, and contain classrooms, lecture rooms, faculty offices, and study centers for student residents. At Saint Mary-of-the-Woods College in Indiana, two or more faculty members live in each hall in the dormitories and maintain counselors' offices in each hall. Utica College of Syracuse University in New York has a program called Encounter whereby a prominent public figure is invited to the campus to live in the dorms for three to five days. The person is usually somewhat controversial. "To date this program has been very successful," says the dean, "but very wearing on the visitor."

Wheaton College in Illinois has provided several facilities within its residence hall to encourage activities other than sleeping and eating. Among these facilities are:

1.   Twelve house lounges available for "bull sessions," for faculty-student interaction, for study
2.   A seminar room available for classroom use and for evening panel discussions
3.   A small library
4.   A fine arts room
5.   Small offices provided for professor-student conferences
6.   Special typing rooms

The existing philosophy which undergirds Wheaton's residence hall program is summarized as follows:

Residence halls at Wheaton College stand as a monument to the conviction that the requisite experiences of a Christian liberal arts education are not confined to the walls of the classroom, laboratory, or library, but touch the whole person in all his experiences. Education, rightly conceived, makes little distinction between the formal curriculum and the learning opportunities outside the classroom. It stresses the necessity of totally enveloping the student in a climate of learning. . . . The residence is not conceived, then, as a haven of escape from the rigorous discipline of scholarly work, but rather as a unique center of learning where the students' academic pursuits take on new dimensions. It is our intent that residence halls will provide an environment wherein the student can select, create, and encounter an array of learning experiences which will, in a significant way, contribute to his total development. Our desire is that the physical facilities, staff, and program of the halls will create for the residents a level of expectancy and climate of learning which will have profound consequences in their lives both on and off the campus.

Students in the New Division of Nasson College in Maine last fall moved into a living-learning center. Men live in one wing of a V-shaped building, women in the other, and between them are lounges, seminar rooms, and classrooms. The design of the new residence halls at Beloit College in Wisconsin includes a number of small seminar-lounge areas in which professors meet with students on an informal basis. These lounges also serve as spots where small groups of students can gather to continue a class discussion or invite outside persons to meet with them to brainstorm a particular subject. Beloit is now undertaking a study, with the cooperation of a student committee, to make the dormitories even greater learning centers than they currently are. All seven dormitories constructed during the last seven years at Claremont Men's College in California include a faculty residence to bring faculty members into closer contact with students. These faculty residents have no responsibility of any kind for the operation of the dormitories or for any discipline in connection therewith. The faculty member's function is entirely one of relations with students as they develop in a normal fashion. Each of the halls includes a lounge where student-faculty discussions are held. Classes and seminars have been held in the residence lounges only to a limited extent in the past, but specific consideration of this question is occurring at this time with the likelihood of increased use of dormitories for instruction in the near future.

Messiah College in Pennsylvania has received a $10,000 grant from the United States Office of Education to study possible cooperative relationships with other educational institutions. One of the results of this study is the genuine possibility of establishing a Messiah College Living-Learning Center on the campus of a large university.

Such a center would serve two groups of Messiah College students: selected upper-division students would attend for a university semester experience after which they would return to continue their programs on the base campus at Grantham; and students interested in finishing certain curricula which could be begun but not finished at Messiah College, such as physics and engineering. At the Living-Learning Center, students would enroll for general education studies offered by Messiah College; they would enroll concurrently in the university for advanced course work.

The Messiah College faculty authorized a university Living-Learning Center pilot project to be launched in September 1968. Such a project envisions a pilot group of from fifteen to thirty students and three or four faculty members. This faculty would team-teach a general education program geared especially to exploration of the implications of the confrontation of Messiah College Christian value commitments with the life of a secular university, preferably a university located in an urban center. The concept of this project has the warm support of the Middle States Association of Colleges and Secondary Schools, the Pennsylvania Department of Public Instruction, and the United States Office of Education.

Several colleges have introduced, or are planning to introduce, technological equipment to bring instructional capabilities to the dormitories. The dean of La Salle College in Pennsylvania reports that "our plan is a long-range one and involves installing TV monitors as learning stations. Presently we use the residence halls lounges for occasional discussion." At Lock Haven State College in Pennsylvania, plans call for installing coaxial cable in all the living centers so that students may view taped lectures at times other than the regularly scheduled classes. In addition, plans call for a computerized dial access system tied in with the library for information retrieval. Ithaca College in New York has installed study carrels and computer terminals in its new dormitories so that individual study capabilities are now available to students. Florida Atlantic provides carrel spaces in the dormitories, and also has television sets within the dormitories making campus closed-circuit programs available.

Of the 200 institutions who responded that they use the dormitory as a learning center, few of them approach the futuristic concept of the dormitory. The college dormitory of the future will cease to be for housing alone, but will be an important adjunct of the teaching and learning process. Today's dormitory room is primarily for sleep and study; tomorrow's will be a complete learning cell, likely to include:

1. A television playback screen, so the student can review portions of lectures, discussions, and laboratory work.

2. Computerized library retrieval. Using a device in his room, the student will electronically request research information, which will be instantly printed out. The library itself will become a huge computer memory core.

3. Screen projection of textbooks. The student will do his reading on viewing screens, dialing the book and page he wants.

4. Language laboratory facilities. Each room will be equipped with tapes, headphones, and tape recorder for foreign language study.

5. Sleep-teaching equipment. Audio facilities will be connected to a pillow speaker, so the student can learn while sleeping.

6. Voice-actuated typewriter. Instead of writing out notes or term papers, the student will speak into a microphone connected to a typewriter that will produce clean, legible copy.

In addition, futurists predict that there will be more "livability" features provided. Among these will be convertible built-in furniture to permit the room to be converted from learning cell to pleasant living room; physical conditioning equipment including ultraviolet lamps and isometric exercise equipment; piped-in music; electrostatic cleaning; and commercial television.

All the items mentioned are already available.

COMPREHENSIVE EXAMINATIONS

In an attempt to offset the mistaken notion that knowledge comes packaged in course units and that a course taken is automatically assimilated, liberal arts colleges have been using comprehensive examinations for a long time. (See Table 3.)

At Macalester College in Minnesota, the faculty in 1967 adopted an extensive statement of policy and procedure concerning comprehensive examinations which are representative of the approaches taken in this area by many colleges in the United States. The faculty at Macalester feel that a senior comprehensive examination may have several very desirable consequences in the total educational program of Macalester College. The senior comprehensive is an examination in a student's concentration, and as such can contribute to those goals toward which the concentration program itself is aimed. Foremost among these is

the goal of ensuring that each graduating student has a competence in some recognized discipline, a competence which brings him near the frontiers of knowledge and accomplishment in the discipline and gives him a sense of being able to carry on a meaningful, if limited, dialogue with others working at those frontiers.

In addition, the faculty feel that a comprehensive examination, to the extent that it demands interrelating of materials within the discipline and calls for knowledge and insight gained from thought and reading outside courses themselves, may greatly increase the likelihood that interrelations will be sought. Moreover, a comprehensive examination encourages the student to adopt study attitudes and techniques which enhance longerterm retention and assimilation than might otherwise be obtained. The comprehensive examination places a common target before the student and the faculty. In summary,

an effective senior comprehensive examination program encourages the student to take greater responsibility for his education in his chosen area of concentration, increases the likelihood that certain valued outcomes of such specialization will be realized, and provides a climax to his Macalester years.

The Macalester program uses visiting examiners who participate with the college faculty in the examination. The faculty feel that several benefits tend to offset the administrative complications of such participation. First, the participation of an outside examiner tends to ensure that the comprehensive examination will not merge with or become simply a glorified substitute for final course examinations. Second, a program which includes an outside examiner provides a structure in which faculty members become the intellectual guides and counselors of students who face the challenge of demonstrating to a visiting examiner their knowledge of their area of concentration. Third, such a program extends valuable opportunities for faculty members to share teaching and curricular ideas with visiting colleagues in the context of observing the performance of students at the completion of their Macalester work.

Each major or core department administers a written comprehensive examination to its core and major students. It is recommended, but not required, that an oral examination also be administered. At the discretion of the department, "standardized" tests such as the GRE Advanced Test may be incorporated into the comprehensive examination. The content of the comprehensive examination is broader than the specific courses which a student has taken. It is the responsibility of each department to inform its students when they enter the core or major program as to the coverage of the comprehensive examination which the student will face as a senior.

To avoid conflicting conceptions of how the conventional letter grades should be applied to the comprehensive examination, Macalester uses a grading system of Pass with highest distinction, Pass with distinction, Pass, and Fail. The grade appears on the student's transcript. Students who fail the comprehensive may retake it at the next scheduled examination period. A makeup examination must be passed within one year of the original examination.

The pattern at Macalester is the pattern at many of the liberal arts colleges that use a comprehensive examination. Haverford College in

Pennsylvania requires each senior to take a special major comprehensive examination (written, oral, or both), the purpose being to "promote the student's comprehension, integration and application of the knowledge acquired in the field of his major concentration, and to secure evidence of this achievement." Windham College in Vermont, Dominican College in Wisconsin, Allegheny College in Pennsylvania, Carroll College in Montana, and many others all require a senior comprehensive examination on the pattern of Macalester and Haverford. The comprehensive examination program at Beloit College in Wisconsin is designed more as a comprehensive evaluation of the student's work than as a strict examination in his particular discipline. Thus, in addition to testing the student on a major field, the examination (evaluation) asks the student to relate his discipline to other areas and to some of the ethical questions facing society today. Similarly, the faculty of Dunbarton College of Holy Cross in Washington, D.C., feel that the comprehensive examination

should be constructed with a view not so much toward measuring quantitatively the student's competence in the courses she has taken as toward testing her power to apply her entire intellectual experience in a unified way to problems and topics which require the broadened approach to which she was introduced in her reading list course and coordinating seminar. It should also test her ability to extemporize on propositions and problems she has not seen before in the form presented in the examination.

Other colleges use comprehensive examinations as a feature of the honors program. At the College of Letters and Science at the University of California, Berkeley, an honors student takes one or more courses of individual study in his senior year to prepare himself for the comprehensive examination.

Variations in Grading Practices

The variation in grading most commonly reported by colleges was the Pass–Fail grading option. The option permits a student to receive a pass or a fail evaluation for work done in a course instead of a letter grade. College faculties adopt the Pass–Fail grade system in the hope that the student will become more aware of the value of learning for its own sake and that there will be less inclination to learn for the sake of securing grades. The option is designed to encourage the student who wishes to venture into a field of knowledge relatively unknown or difficult without the fear that unsatisfactory performance will impair his academic standing.

The Pass–Fail option is in effect at such colleges as Bennington in

Vermont, Brown in Rhode Island, Mount Holyoke in Massachusetts, Princeton, Queens College in New York, San Jose State College in California, and the College of Arts and Science at the University of California at Berkeley. Most colleges permit students to take only one Pass–Fail course each term, with the restriction that the course be outside the student's major field. For example, at Lindenwood College, Missouri, with the exception of the freshman student who is enrolled in her first term at Lindenwood, any student who has at least a 2.0 grade-point average and is carrying a normal load, including the Pass–Fail course, is eligible for the Pass–Fail option. Only three requirements in any way limit the student's freedom to elect the Pass–Fail option: (1) Only one Pass–Fail course may be taken in any one term; (2) No more than five Pass–Fail courses will be recorded on the student's scholastic record and counted among the thirty-four courses required for graduation; (3) The Pass–Fail option may not be utilized in divisional or departmental course requirements, or for courses in the student's area of concentration. At Colgate in New York, students with junior or senior standing, who have been accepted in a field of concentration, may elect to take one course a semester in which the course is evaluated Pass or Fail instead of by the usual letter grades. Berkeley also limits the Pass–Fail option to no more than one course in each quarter. The units earned by passing courses count toward the degree but are disregarded in computing the student's grade-point average.

In January 1967, the Faculty Council at Brooklyn College of the City University of New York voted to institute a Pass–Fail program on an experimental basis for two years beginning in the fall of 1967. The following were the procedures and guidelines which governed the Pass-Fail option.

1. Juniors and seniors may elect one course each semester, summer excluded, on a Pass–Fail basis. The maximum number of such courses is four.

2. A course elected on a Pass–Fail basis must be one which is elective for a student and which falls outside his major department.

3. The selection of a Pass–Fail course can only be made during the first two-weeks of the semester. Once a student has selected a course on a Pass–Fail basis, he is not permitted to change to the *A* to *F* grading basis.

4. Honors courses are excluded from the Pass–Fail program.

The Committee on Course and Standing at Brooklyn College emphasizes that Pass–Fail grading plans are designed to "encourage a student to explore areas of inherent interest and thus achieve greater breadth of view." The committee feels that a student often hesitates to take courses in new areas since he has no way to gauge his capabilities in such areas. Since maintaining the best possible grade average is of paramount importance to most students, many are reluctant to attempt such exploration if the course is graded *A* through *F*.

Some colleges have introduced a Satisfactory–Unsatisfactory option rather than Pass–Fail. Kenyon College in Ohio, Allegheny College in Pennsylvania, and Earlham College in Indiana are examples of colleges adopting this system. At Earlham the plan provides that (1) a passing grade of *S* (Satisfactory) represents work of *C* level or higher and a failing grade of *U* (Unsatisfactory) represents work below *C* level; (2) *S* and *U* grades will be recorded but not included in computation of grade-point averages; (3) juniors and seniors who wish to elect this option must indicate their choice within the first week of the term.

The College of Liberal Arts of Drake University, Iowa, in addition to instituting a program of Pass–Fail, permits any student to pay a $10 fee and take an examination for any course in the university for credit. Conceivably a student could earn a degree through this method.

The College of Liberal Arts of the University of Minnesota, and Westminster College in Missouri, have slight variations in the grading practices. At Minnesota, the faculty approved a *P–N* (Pass–No Credit) grading system which exists side-by-side with the *A–F* system. A student, at the beginning of a quarter, can elect to take up to one-third of his work in *P–N* courses. Once committed he cannot shift to the other grading system. Westminster College in 1965 eliminated the *A* through *F* grading system and substituted the following: *DN*—Distinction; *HP*—High Pass; and *P*—Pass.

According to the dean of Westminster College, three dominant purposes promoted the changing of grade categories: (1) The college wished its pattern of grading, widely varied according to individual teacher and department, to become more consistent; (2) The college sought to raise standards in particular ways—through narrowing the top category and through eliminating the *D* range; (3) By eliminating the *F* grade, removing its everlasting punishment for not succeeding, and by actively rewarding only satisfactory work, the college sought to eliminate some evils indigenous to the old system—the practices of avoiding hard courses, taking only subjects in which one can do well, taking light loads, and so on. The college now keeps an "institutional memory" of "No Credit" reports, but these are no part of the official student records.

By now the dean's office of Westminster has looked at considerably more than 10,000 grades, and has run several detailed computer analyses. As a result, the dean of the college maintains that clear-cut evidence has established that the college is significantly more con-sistent in its grading policies than it was before, and there is complete un-coerced agreement in the meaning of the various marks. . . . The effect upon student motivation of eliminating *"F"* grades can be assessed in various ways, . . . at this stage it can only be reported that the college is not ready to report, though of course it is working from a research design. See us a year from now, and, periodically, later on.

Fordham College, Bronx, New York, began the Pass–Fail system in the spring of 1967 and "has found it moderately successful to date." Sophomores, juniors, and seniors are allowed to choose one course on the Pass–Fail basis during each semester. The course chosen, however, may not be taken either from the core curriculum or from the field of the student's major concentration. According to the dean, the purpose in in-stituting the system was to make the students

more venturesome, going into fields which they felt might hurt their overall index. I have a feeling that we have not really attained this purpose. I have not noticed many English majors taking heavier mathematics courses. A good number of our students, however, have taken advantage of the system but we are really rethinking the whole program.

At Goucher College in Maryland, an *ad hoc* student-faculty Commit-tee on Records held a series of meetings dealing with ways to deepen the meaning of a student's educational experience. The committee inquired as closely as it was able into the Princeton Plan as well as into those that are close kin to it at Knox College in Illinois and Carleton College in Min-nesota. Princeton opens the plan to all students to the extent of one Pass–Fail course a year, but with courses in the junior and senior years re-stricted to those outside the major. At Knox the plan is hedged about with a good many restrictions: it is open only to juniors and seniors with a *C* average; the courses that can be elected must be outside the major and cannot include any that would fall in the category of college require-ments for graduation, that is, distribution, foreign language, or English requirements. At Carleton the plan is open to students who have had fifteen Carleton courses and allows the election of one Pass–Fail course a term up to a limit of seven courses. The Goucher committee indicated that they were in agreement with the underlying objectives of the Prince-ton, Knox, and Carleton plans but the committee is also deeply interest-ed in finding out whether an ungraded course situation releases "educa-tional motivations that tend to be imprisoned in a graded situation. This is why our recommendations, particularly as they apply to freshmen and sophomores, go somewhat farther than the plans at Princeton, Knox, and Carleton."

The *ad hoc* committee anticipated that one response to their recommendations would be to argue that if students do not have to think about grades in certain courses they will do less work in them and receive proportionately less education. The report continued:

But this is by no means a foregone conclusion. Other results are conceivable. We think it at least possible that many students will profit as much from taking a course without being graded in it as they would under ordinary circumstances. Or, if they do not put as much effort into such a course, they may well develop greater interest in the remaining graded courses or perhaps turn their attention to endeavors that are academically rewarding even if they are not under faculty supervision and thus not strictly speaking curricular.

Against the fear that graduate schools and other interested parties may look askance at records lacking the usual complement of letter grades, the *ad hoc* committee indicated that

it is difficult to believe that conventional grades in more than three quarters of the courses a student takes in four years plus letters of recommendation would not adequately indicate a student's ability; the grade of Pass in the other courses would at least indicate areas covered.

The associate dean of Trinity College, Connecticut, where the Pass–Fail option has been introduced, indicates his cynicism about the advantage of the option, and states "I believe that I notice a rather marked trend amongst the lower ranking students to elect a course under it which they would have taken anyhow, but in which they would not have expected to do too well." Another dean of a liberal arts college indicated that he knew of no variations in grading practices "other than via the idiosyncrasy of the individual teachers." At Stanford in California, a senior honors student did a senior essay on the "Pass–Fail Option—an Evaluation of the Stanford Experience." The Pass–Fail grading option was introduced at Stanford University in the autumn quarter of 1966. The evaluation study found that 18 per cent of the undergraduate student body elected a course on a Pass–Fail basis, and that courses were elected from almost all departments. According to instructors, Pass–Fail students worked hard, but did not perform as well as graded students. Students chose Pass–Fail because they were insecure about the course subject matter, did not want to spend as much time on the course, wanted to determine their independence from grade motivations, or were curious about the course. Pass–Fail students felt they learned as much as they would have, had they taken the course for a grade, although they reported working less hard. Students overwhelmingly reported that they enjoyed the courses more, and most intended to take other courses on a Pass–Fail basis. Twenty-five per cent of the students indicated that they took courses on a Pass–Fail basis that they would not have taken otherwise.

A joint faculty-student committee at Stonehill College in Massachusetts recently adopted a new grading system, the major feature of which provides that freshman grades are not included in the over-all graduation average. The student must do well enough to be admitted to the sophomore class but his marks are not counted in his cumulative average. In effect, the student begins his sophomore year with a clean slate without being forced to live with low grades that he might have received in his early college days. Besides giving the student a fresh chance at his graduation average, the new system has the added advantage of facilitating a change in a major program. A student may find, during his freshman year, that he prefers or has more aptitude for a different program than his original choice. He now can make this changeover without being saddled with any low grades resulting from his initial efforts.

To encourage students to experiment with courses outside their major field, the new system at Stonehill also grants students a Pass–Fail grade option.

Chapter 4

NEW POSITION OF STUDENTS ON CAMPUS

STUDENT ACTIONS, SPEECHES, AND INFORMAL SEMINARS MAKE IT CLEAR that students across the country are demanding broad changes in what they learn and how they learn it. In addition, students are seeking a greater voice in administrative as well as academic issues on their own campuses. One manifestation of student discontent has been the increasing demand for student participation on faculty committees that evaluate curriculums, give tenure to professors, and set rules for student life.

The events at Columbia University in 1968 are a very dramatic illustration of student discontent. At Douglass College in New Jersey students threatened a lawsuit to gain a larger voice in the decision-making process. At Yale, students went on strike when a popular teacher was discharged and demanded the right to participate in the selection of professors. At Brown University in Rhode Island students have drafted a radical plan for reform of the curriculum that involves the virtual elimination of grades and the end to formal departmental structure, which they believe is a barrier to a broad understanding of society.

Other significant changes are occurring at Brown University. Students, in the past, have not played any formal role in the governance of Brown. Last fall, however, they began to do so insofar as the entire area of social rules and regulations is concerned, following the adoption by the Brown Corporation of the Magrath Report.[1] In addition to a new

[1] C. Peter Magrath, Chairman, "Community and Partnership: Student Conduct at Brown University." Report of the Advisory Committee on Student Conduct. May, 1967. (Mimeographed.)

University Council on Student Affairs, undergraduates at Brown, effective last fall, were appointed to a reorganized Housing Committee for the college, a committee which will make policy recommendations to the president concerning the residential system at Brown, off-campus housing, and related matters. Last spring, President Heffner of Brown appointed two student representatives, with full voting power, to a special *ad hoc* committee to investigate the university's procedures and policies with regard to the whole general area of confidentiality of student records with special attention to the release of information concerning students to draft boards and prospective employers.

Some students have gone outside the formal university structure to start free universities and experimental colleges, which now operate as extracurricular activities on the fringes of from forty to sixty campuses. Some of the experimental colleges have formal courses. Some are sanctioned by a university. San Francisco State in California even gives credit to students who complete the courses. Others prefer to be independent and, like Dartmouth College in New Hampshire, involve local residents. Mike Vozick, a leader in the educational reform movement at San Francisco State College and who organized the first experimental college at San Francisco State two years ago, explained that the purpose of the schools was "not only to teach subjects that are not given in the universities, but to explore new ways of learning." [2] The basic purpose of these attempts at experimentation outside the formal university structure is to force changes within the established institutions, rather than to create and perpetuate new ones.

STUDENT INVOLVEMENT IN GOVERNANCE

The history of the student attempt to participate in university governance did not begin with the Berkeley riots. Even if we disregard the tremendous power wielded by students at medieval universities, we can still relate present-day concerns over student participation to the early decades of this century. It was in the 1920's, 1930's, and 1940's that places such as Antioch and Denison in Ohio, Sarah Lawrence in New York, Bennington in Vermont, and Bard in New York placed considerable responsibility in the hands of students regarding every conceivable area of academic life. True, the motivation for such activity was somewhat different from the present scene, for in these early days there appeared to be mutual faculty, administration, and student concern for the development of creative leadership potential in a democratic society, which in turn required the highest

[2] *New York Times,* August 20, 1967, p. 38.

degree of creative self-exploration, unfettered by inflexible rules imposed from without. Today, the motivating forces are substantially different, ranging from the publicly expressed, unabashed search for a share of campus power affluency, through strong desires for self-regulation and self-determination, to the very high reaches of altruism involved in the search for personal responsibility in areas of meaningful activity. There are many indications that this latter motive inspires a good deal of present student interest in participation. "To frustrate this urge," suggests a Catholic college *ad hoc* committee on student participation, "may very well result in a greater sense of the alienation and anomie, which play a large part in current student unrest and rebellion."[3]

The alleged obstacles to student representation should not be minimized. Obstacles which are often mentioned are:

1. Students are immature and are lacking in experience appropriate to such responsibilities.

2. They have a short-term connection with the college, which means that present action does not carry with it subsequent responsibility.

3. The task of educating new student representatives to the nature and policies of the committees would be an added burden on faculty members, and the extent of student willingness and ability to devote the time to committee work is questionable.

Several colleges indicated that students ask for more responsibility but then do not want to do the work. "Student pressure to participate in college governance is increasing slightly," said one dean, "but our experience has been that relatively few students are willing to really do the work." Another dean reported that recently his faculty formally voted to extend to students an invitation to designate two of their members as voting members of the faculty Committee on Admissions and Student Aid. To date, "the students have expressed preference for forgoing such participation, chiefly on the ground that they cannot spare the time that would be required for the full involvement which would have to accompany voting privileges."

There is still another group of college administrators and faculty that feels that there are limits to be placed in respect to the actual delegation of power and authority to students. William T. Higdon, president of Graceland College, Iowa, and Charles C. Cole, Jr., provost and dean of Lafayette College, Pennsylvania, are representative of this group. Higdon ac-

[3] *Ad hoc* Committee on Student Participation Report to Faculty and Students of Saint Xavier College, May 5, 1967. (Mimeographed.)

cepts student membership in committees such as the concert, convocation, health and safety, library, student aid, and student life council, and suggests they should have full voting powers. He states:

There are other committees and councils where we doubt the advisability of student participation. Among these are the curricular adjustment committee, responsible for decision making regarding course load adjustment, academic probation and academic suspension. We feel that there are two where we must be especially careful as we consider the possibility of student participation. The academic council, in addition to having primary responsibility in curriculum development, also has frequent occasion to discuss the academic situation of individual students. We question whether students should be present during these discussions. . . . The other is the council on student welfare which often handles very delicate matters involving student offenses, where confidentiality may be highly desirable.

Cole of Lafayette College put it this way:

Lafayette College has an enrollment of 1700 undergraduates. We are, therefore, in a position to do some things which are not practical on a larger campus. We seek to encourage students to look upon their college as a community and to give faculty members and administrative officers the benefit of their ideas and opinions. We do a number of things which are aimed at reducing that traditional gap between the students and the so-called "administration." We seek to encourage students to participate in the life of the community. However, I think there is a limit in respect to the actual delegation of power and authority to students. I think that some of the problems in colleges and universities today are the result of a failure by students, faculty and administrative officers to recognize such limits. Student opinion in curricular matters should be solicited by the faculty member and administrator. Student ideas with respect to teaching, subject matter, credits and grades and other topics related to their education can be very useful, very valuable. However, the student is the student, the learner, the inexperienced and uninformed. He or she cannot possibly have the expertness or perspective to make decisions involving fundamental changes in the curriculum. An adolescent probably would hesitate to advise his doctor on medical matters, his lawyer on legal matters. Why then does he assume that his professor lacks the necessary qualities to decide on curricular matters? Student opinion should be sought but I have strong reservations about involving students in the legislative and organizational process by which curricular matters are decided.

Nevertheless, the evidence would seem to indicate that a growing number of liberal arts colleges recognize the possible advantages of student representation and that this would appear to outweigh these alleged disadvantages. It is a growing opinion of college administrators and faculty that some form of student representation on faculty committees is desirable and for varied reasons.

1.   It would ensure greater communication and understanding between student, faculty, and administration. The importance of the constant full and free flow of information and ideas between the various community levels for establishing a deep sense of solidarity and common life cannot be overstressed. Such communal feeling may in our time be the principal source of the inspiration for intellectual achievement.

2.   The college would benefit from the students' contribution to policy within the college. In many cases, the more responsible and creative students can provide fresh insights of startling relevance into the academic undertaking. Many students are strongly dedicated to the pursuit of skills and objective scholarship, and many have a kind of personal loyalty to their college that some faculty members, in light of their commitment to a wider professional community, sometimes cannot experience.

3.   Students would gain experience from a more active and responsible role in the government of the college. When students desire to participate responsibly in the government of the institution they attend, their wish should be recognized as a claim to opportunity for an educational experience. Students expect that the educational process will be so structured that they will be stimulated by it to learn to function effectively and to develop qualities of leadership in a democratic society, that the cultural heritage of the larger society will be effectively transmitted to them, and that they will gain the experience of exercising the virtues demanded of them by that society as the mark of maturity.

4.   Students would gain unique personal satisfaction in helping guide an institution of which they are a part. The process of maturation in the college student, as in any human being, involves a change from a passive and accepting attitude to an active, vital, and responsibly critical role in the college community. A student's feelings of discontent, disinterest, and frustration are symptoms of being faced with an institution which he feels he cannot influence; sometimes this is because he has not himself made the transition to a responsibly active role. Student representation would provide a stimulus for the exercise of critical judgment and a means of responsible influence.

Among representative statements from college officers which illustrate the above points of view are the following:

We have found from past experience that having student membership and giving the students the same voting rights and same privileges as any faculty

member on these councils gives the students a sense of real involvement in decision making. We have found that this is a helpful method of communication
between the administration, the faculty, and the students—*Mayville State
College, North Dakota.*

We find that extension of the privilege of participation on faculty committees to students is immensely helpful in involving them in the college.
Small matters are settled before they can become crises. In addition, it is not
an empty honor. Many of the administrative and academic changes which
have been made at Jamestown College the past three years have been student
initiated. . . . The criticism which we probably hear more often than any other
when telling others of our program is, "What about leakage of confidential information?" We have never had such a situation occur on the part of students.
Ironically, enough, we find that faculty members are quite prone to violation
of confidential material, whereas students, perhaps because of the immensity
of the responsibility, are as closed-mouthed as clams.—*Jamestown College,
North Dakota.*

STUDENT CONDUCT

In surveying the liberal arts college campuses of the country, an attempt was made to discern the various practices that exist to involve
students in institutional governance. The majority of institutions allow
students to run their own organizations and their extracurricular activities, usually with a faculty adviser. Reflecting the belief that those affected by student conduct policies and procedures ought to participate significantly in making and in enforcing these policies, colleges are attempting to achieve a working partnership between the administration, faculty,
and students in the matter of making and enforcing social policies and
student conduct rules. More specifically, colleges are willing to give
students a substantial role in the area of rules-making and rules-enforcing
procedures first, because social and student policies and procedures
impinge directly and almost exclusively on the students, and second,
because students are more likely to act maturely and responsibly within
a social system which they help to create and to enforce.

In surveying the colleges in regard to their practices in this area, the
answers, as expected, revealed a variety of options that one may choose
from in establishing machinery and procedures for making and enforcing
rules. Presumably, each college or university has practices and procedures
that to some considerable degree reflect its particular traditions and needs.
Interestingly, though, three broad trends seem to have emerged.

First, a majority of all the responding institutions reported that students were part of a mechanism primarily responsible for the formulation
of student conduct regulations. Moreover, a large number of schools

(Cornell, Dartmouth, Illinois, North Carolina, Northwestern, Pennsylvania, Stanford, Swarthmore, and Wesleyan) reported that this function was performed by a joint administration-faculty-student board.

Second, a good number of deans reported that students are formally and significantly involved in rendering decisions in the most serious disciplinary cases. Many schools have their own variations, but the two basic patterns are those where responsibility belongs to a faculty-student board or to an administration-faculty-student board. So-called "appeals" procedures also vary greatly, but the most common pattern provides for appeal to the president (Amherst, Antioch, Bryn Mawr, Columbia, Dartmouth, Northwestern, Pennsylvania, Tufts, Morehouse, Vassar, and Williams); another pattern provides for appeal to a dean (Chicago, Mount Holyoke, and Pennsylvania).

Third, the responses suggest that the colleges guarantee certain procedural safeguards to students involved in disciplinary cases. Thus, at some schools, students are notified in writing of the precise charge against them; they may be represented by a faculty member, and may present evidence and witnesses.

SPECIFIC PRACTICES

The *Ad Hoc* Committee on Student Participation, at Saint Xavier College in Illinois, responding to a request from a small but articulate group of students who expressed deep concern over the lack of meaning in the areas and activities of student government and quietly requested consideration of special ways in which students may share meaningfully in the government of the full community, proposed a plan for a College Community Council.

At Dickinson College in Pennsylvania, students have the majority voice in the two judicial bodies of the college, the Student-Faculty Judicial Council and the Social Violations Hearings Board. Matters of academic dishonesty such as plagiarism are referred by professors to the Student-Faculty Judicial Council, which is composed of four students and four members of the faculty. The student members are elected by the Student Senate with the vice-president of the Student Senate serving ex officio. Violations of college special regulations are referred to the Social Violations Hearings Board. This body is composed of three students, one faculty member, and the deans of men and women. Again, the student members are elected by the Student Senate with the vice-president of the Student Senate serving ex officio.

The chief area of responsibility for students at Princeton is in the administration of the Honor System. The faculty must give its approval

TABLE 4 LIBERAL ARTS COLLEGES INVOLVED WITH INNOVATIONS IN THE AREA OF STUDENT GOVERNANCE AND SERVICES

Item	Number of Usable Responses to Item [a]	Percentage of Usable Responses	Before 1961	Percentage of Responses	1961 and After	Percentage of Responses	Planning to Introduce	Percentage of Responses
Student participation on faculty committees	662	75.1	249	37.7	370	55.8	43	6.5
Student involvement in faculty evaluation	540	61.2	212	39.3	274	50.7	54	10.0
Student involvement in faculty selection	23	2.6	4	17.4	19	82.6	—	—
Special examinations for admissions	393	44.6	241	61.3	144	36.7	8	2.0
Other variations in admissions	192	21.8	65	33.9	111	57.8	16	8.3
Early identification of the gifted	235	26.6	113	48.1	104	44.3	18	7.6
Articulation with high schools	584	66.2	417	71.4	145	24.8	22	3.8
Advanced placement	708	80.2	305	43.1	370	52.2	33	4.7

[a] The total number of usable responses to the questionnaire was 882.

to the decisions of the Honor Committee, which consists of seven student representatives. "To my knowledge," said an assistant dean of the college, "it has never contravened or amended the Committee's recommendations since the inception of the Honor System in 1893." In addition, three students appointed by the undergraduate Assembly are voting members of the Faculty Committee on Discipline.

At Brown University in Rhode Island, however, an Advisory Committee on Student Conduct was appointed by President Ray L. Heffner on November 15, 1966, and charged with the broad responsibilities of examining

the relationship between student conduct and the proper atmosphere of a university; to consider the present state of student conduct at Brown University; to examine rules and codes of behavior in The College, Pembroke College, and The Graduate School; to consider the procedures by which such rules and codes are amended and enforced; to make recommendations to the appropriate authorities.

The Advisory Committee, chaired by C. Peter Magrath, an associate professor of political science, reported in May 1967. Sections of the report and specific recommendations made by the Advisory Committee reflect trends in regard to student conduct on American liberal arts college campuses.

The Committee started with some major assumptions.

1.   The Committee felt that it is meaningful to speak of a Brown University community. While they recognized that there were diverse participants within this community, the Corporation, administration, faculty, and students at Brown ultimately share common interests. This University community is an inter-dependent one, with the attitudes and behavior of each of its component groups having an impact on the other participants. As the quality of the faculty affects the welfare of the student body, so too does the quality of life among the students affect other members of the community. On the matter of making and enforcing social policies and student conduct rules, the Committee believed that the University's common interests can best be identified and pursued through a partnership process.

2.   It is equally desirable that the University establish a formal mechanism which can provide a continuous forum for the discussion of the University's social system and which can authoritatively recommend adjustments and changes as experience and needs indicate.

3.   While there are always individual variations, students do not acquire maturity instantaneously upon receiving high school diplomas. It is also true that for many students the first years of college involve significant changes in their environment. Most young people, however, grow toward maturity, and we believe that the wisest response to this process of maturation and adult

socialization is a structure in which negative student conduct rules are gradually and significantly diminished.

4.   The University's emphasis on student conduct matters must, as much as possible, be in the direction of counselling and education. Nonetheless, a university cannot function without some minimal rules intended to keep order, to maintain, as much as possible, "a way of student life that is physically and psychologically healthy, and to preserve satisfactory relations with the larger civil community of which the University is a part." Such minimum rules as are formulated ought to be stated as explicitly as possible. "We are opposed to vague rules such as those contained in phrases that make students liable for 'ungentlemanly conduct,' 'conduct unbecoming to a student' or 'conduct against the best interests of the institution.' "

5.   Catch phrases such as "in loco parentis" confuse rather than clarify the understanding of student conduct questions. The University, while undoubtedly an alma mater to many of its sons and daughters in a certain nostalgic sense, is not equipped to serve as a surrogate parent for its students.

To sum up, the report states that "man is neither wholly good, nor wholly bad. We hope, therefore, that education will bring out the best in man, but we realize that minimal rules and sanctions are necessary to cope with the worst in man." [4]

STUDENT PARTICIPATION IN FACULTY COMMITTEES

One of the significant developments in liberal arts colleges is the growing tendency to involve students in institutional direction. Of the 882 usable responses in the sample, 662 institutions or 75 per cent indicated that students participated on faculty committees. (See Table 4.) What is even more significant, however, is that 360 of the 662, or 54.3 per cent, indicated that they had instituted the practice since 1961. In addition, 43 colleges or 6.5 per cent of the respondees indicated that they were planning to introduce the practice.

Of course, the amount of involvement ranged widely—from colleges where students were highly involved in the governance of their own organizational, social, and extracurricular structures but limited in their involvement in the traditionally "nonstudent" areas, to colleges where students actually were integral parts of key faculty and administrative committees.

The various practices can be grouped as follows.

1.   Students serve on faculty committees but they have no voting rights. They merely serve in an advisory capacity. Typical of this approach is the system at the undergraduate division of Stanford University. Under the rules of the faculty there are no student members on facul-

[4] C. Peter Magrath, *op cit.,* pp. 7–16.

ty committees; rather, a number of these committees have student advisers who sit as committee members on most occasions, but without vote. Virtually all the presidential comittees, however, include student membership. Although students are in every case a minority, they do have full rights. The presidential committees operate as advisors to the president, whereas the faculty committees have certain policy-making rights delegated by the faculty. Presidential committees include athletics, financial aid, foreign visitors and students, public exercises, religious activities, and student affairs and services. Some examples include:

Lake Erie College, Ohio.   Students are consulted, through their leaders and representatives to a Faculty-Student Committee as well as through close relationships with members of the faculty and administration, on many academic and administrative matters. This is not power —elective or authoritative, rights or controls.

State University College at Geneseo, New York.   Students serve in an advisory, nonvoting capacity on two of the faculty committees which recommend policy to the president of the college. Specifically, the Faculty Senate Committee on Student Affairs consists of twelve faculty senators and six students. The committee meets weekly during the school year and "recommends to the Executive Committee of the Senate general policy relating to the admissions, scholarship, and placement of students; social and extracurricular activities of the College; allocation of financial aids available to students; student rights and responsibilities." Students also serve as nonvoting advisers to the Faculty Senate Committee on Undergraduate Academic Affairs. This committee consists of thirteen faculty and four students.

Bucknell University, Pennsylvania.   Although students do not serve as members on regular university committees, they are used quite frequently for consultation. For example, the Student Committee on Academic Affairs, a standing committee of student government, is frequently consulted by the Curriculum Committee of the College of Arts and Sciences.

Westmar College, Iowa.   The student governing body is represented by two persons who are selected each year from the students to attend the regular meetings of the Faculty Senate. Except for executive sessions of the Faculty Senate these students are permitted to attend all the meetings and may engage in discussion of any question which is offered. They do not have voting power. According to the dean, "the Westmar experience in relating students to the governance of the college has been very satisfactory. Students have been made to feel that they are welcome to express their viewpoints."

2. By far the most common pattern among the liberal arts colleges is to have student representatives on faculty committees which deal with matters such as athletics, concerts, convocations, library, scholarship, special events, college union matters, religious life, financial aid, student welfare and, as mentioned earlier in the report, on discipline committees. They have equal voting powers with the faculty members. Students are not represented on committees which deal with educational plans and policies.

Tusculum College, Tennessee. Students serve on four of seven committees of the faculty—athletic, campus life, cultural affairs, and religious life. They are voting members on a par with faculty. They are not members of the Executive Committee, Admissions and Academic Standards, and Curriculum. The president of the college appoints the student members from nominations submitted by the president of the Student Government Association. A member of the student body, usually the editor of the student newspaper, is also invited to attend every meeting of the faculty.

Bridgewater College, Virginia. Student representatives serve on faculty committees such as the Council on Student Affairs, the Council on Religious Activities, the Council on Athletics, and the Committee on Convocations. However, there is no student representative on the Council on Administration or on the Council on Education (Curriculum).

3. In the parallel committee system each faculty committee has a corresponding student committee. The parallel committees meet together periodically, sharing ideas and programs. Decisions, however, are still made by the administration, faculty, and trustees. The dean of the College at Ottawa University in Kansas, which uses this system, feels that the system "involves more students and takes the heat off individuals." The Academics Committee at Maryville College in Tennessee, the student counterpart of the faculty Curriculum Committee, is worthy of mention. The Academics Committee has worked closely with the Curriculum Committee in development of programs, and on occasion they meet together.

4. Students are on the key councils and committees of the college with full voting rights. Typical of this approach are Antioch College in Ohio and Reed College in Oregon. At Antioch, students and faculty jointly administer the college's "Community Government"—the organization which in part fills the role of traditional student governments at

many colleges. In addition to decision-making power over such items as hall hours, behavioral standards, and the administration of a $100,000 budget representing the $50 Community Government fee, paid by faculty and students alike, Community Government also has undertaken to deal in matters more appropriately called "educational," by virtue of the college charter which grants to Community Government "all the power it can effectively and responsibly handle." Thus, in recent years, Community Council, the six-student, three–faculty member Community Government administrative board, has hired former S.D.S. leader, Carl Ogelsby, as an "Activist Scholar in Residence"; has provided facilities for the production of both still and moving pictures; and has sponsored courses, taught by students, with academic credit granted by the college, in film making. In addition, students are also involved thoroughly on all levels of decision making in academic matters, both in the setting of policy and in the application of policy to various situations. Three students, elected for one-year terms in community-wide elections, sit as full voting members of the eight-person Administrative Council, chaired by the president of the college. Each of these students is a "full member" of at least several Administrative Council subcommittees, including those organized to review and revise faculty salaries, faculty tenure, faculty sabbatical applications, the college budget, and so on. All three participate in interviewing and deciding whether to hire candidates for the faculty, as well as in contract renewal discussions.

Numerous other students, selected by a process of self-nomination, recommendation of the community manager (a student-held, full time "co-op" position), and approval of the chairmen of the respective committees, are "full members" of virtually every decision-making body in the institution, including the Student Personnel Committee, the Educational Policy Committee, various departmental review committees, and assorted *ad hoc* groups.

At Reed College, students participate in institutional policy making by serving as members of the Community Senate and by sitting on most of the major committees of the faculty. The senate consists of eleven faculty members, elected by the faculty, and ten students, elected by the student body. The senate deals with matters of general community concern such as the Honor Principle, and in the applications and violations thereof; rules governing intervisitation and other behavior in the dormitory; speaker and organization policy for the campus; and so on. Some of these matters may be taken up by the full senate, while a good many others are handled by its subcommittees. In general, matters dealt with by the senate do not come before the faculty or before the faculty's own standing committees. The regular standing committees of the faculty, a few of which are elective and most of which are appointed by the president, tend in general to deal with matters of a more strictly educational nature. Students sit on the very important Educational Policies Committee, the Admissions and Financial Aid Policy Committee, and the Library Board. Students are elected to these seats by the student body. They have a full voice and a full vote in committee proceedings. The assistant to the president at Reed College stated:

The above description may answer your question about their authority though it does not necessarily speak to the question of power. That is a somewhat more difficult matter to define, though I should add that on virtually all of the faculty committees where there is student representation, faculty members do outnumber students. I might also add that the system seems to have achieved for us reasonably effective means of communication between faculty and students.

William H. Schechter, president of Tarkio College in Missouri, suggests that in some ways his college has gone farther in the area of student involvement than any other school in the country. In 1966, the Board of Directors gave approval to seat students on all the key councils and committees of the college with full voting rights. Faculty members and administrative staff are also on all these councils and all members are on an equivalent basis with respect to voting. In June 1967, the Administrative Council was chaired by a student who then became Student Council president. In the fall of 1966, the Student Council president attended a long-range planning conference where six or eight board members met with an equal number of administrators from the college. In April 1967, the Board of Directors elected a student representative and a faculty member to the Board, both to serve ex officio without vote, the same status the president of Tarkio enjoys. Thus, Tarkio has six ex-officio board members without vote: president of the college, president of the Alumni Association, president of the Parents Organization, member of the state church body, a faculty member, and a student.

Other interesting examples of student participation in governance are as follows:

Talladega College, Alabama. The College Council, organized in 1936, has for its purpose "to think together on problems of common concern to the college family; and when general agreement has been reached to formulate policies pertaining to college life, which shall be presented to the Board of Trustees, when necessary." The College Council has been the main governing body on the campus since 1938. Any student or organization may place an item on the agenda of the council but this must be done not later than twenty-four hours preceding the meeting. The meetings of the council are open to all members of the college family, who are free to participate in debating any proposal presented; however, only council members have voting power. The College Council is organized as follows, each member having one vote:

Permanent chairman: The President of the College.

Permanent members: Dean of Instruction, Business Manager, Adviser to Men Students, Counselor of Women Students, Superintendent of Buildings and Grounds.

Six faculty representatives: Elected for a one-year term by the faculty itself.

Six student representatives: One male and one female representative from each of the three upper classes are elected by their respective classes to serve a term of one yar.

Loretto Heights College, Colorado.   This past year, in order to facilitate innovation, the Office of Research and Experimentation won approval from the Curriculum Committee to provide a way of permitting students or faculty the opportunity to initiate ideas for curricular change. The procedure was such that any person wishing to have an idea considered would submit it to the director of the Office of Research and Experimentation and the director would then call an *ad hoc* committee together, made up of faculty and students most apt to be involved and/or to have qualifications about the decision. Students on these *ad hoc* committees were full-fledged members. Some experimental changes reviewed by these *ad hoc* committees, and approved, included Pass–Fail options; credit for off-campus experience; special seminars.

Mundelein College, Illinois.   During 1966–67 two student-faculty committees, one on academic affairs, the other on cultural affairs, were active and effective in changing college policy and assisting in decision making. During the academic year 1967–68, three student members with full voting rights were members of the powerful Academic Board of the College, joining fourteen members of the faculty and three members of the administration. As Vice-President Hruby describes these changes, "Mundelein is in flux!"

Claremont Men's College, California.   Students participate in *ad hoc* committees involving basic policy and also are members of most policy-making faculty committees as distinguished from administrative committees. Students are full-fledged members of committees and have one representative if the faculty members number five or less, and two representatives if faculty members number six or more. Student committee members are appointed by the president of the college, normally from a slate of students presented to him, the slate containing twice the number of students as the number to be appointed. The slate of students is selected by the student members of the Student-Faculty Committee whose student members are appointed by the Student Council.

Jamestown College, North Dakota.   Most Jamestown College committees consist of three students and five faculty members. Students have traveled extensively in connection with their committee memberships, accompanying members of the faculty to various professional meetings and to other regional and national gatherings.

Earlham College, Indiana.   Earlham students, selected by the student government, have been sitting in on the deliberations of a number of faculty committees for several years. Like so many things at Earlham, however, this arrangement was an informal one until 1967, when the faculty formally approved the policy of students being regular members of faculty committees, with the exception of the Faculty Affairs Committee, the Faculty Seminar Committee, and the Nominating Committee. Each student member of faculty committees must have participated in a seminar on college operations given each fall. This seminar is open to all interested students, and is required of students who will serve on faculty committees. "It is noteworthy," said the vice president of academic affairs and dean of the college, "that we follow Quaker business procedure in all committee meetings and faculty meetings at Earlham. This means that no votes are taken and we seek for consensus on the part of all members. The student voice on the committees is significant and influential."

College of Letters and Science, University of California, Berkeley.   Approximately one-half (about twenty) of the departments in the college have mechanisms to facilitate the airing of student grievances and to involve students in consultation with faculty in the area of course revision, curricular requirements, and major programs. In recent years a place has been reserved on the agenda of every meeting of the Academic Senate for the presentation of a communication by the president of the Associated Students. Proposals for student membership on committees of the Academic Senate are presently under consideration by a Commission on University Governance, consisting of faculty members and student representatives.

5. Students are allowed contact with boards of trustees either by appointment on a formal basis to attend meetings, or by invitation to attend on special occasions. This practice is not very common and appears to have developed in recent years. At Central Washington State College the president of the Student Government Association is an ex-officio member of the President's Council, the top administrative organization of the college, and attends all meetings of the Board of Trustees. In both instances, the student president has the right to participate in discussion but not to vote. At Otterbein College in Ohio, Presiden Lynn W. Turner reports that

. . . in the last ten years we have invited students elected by the Student Senate to participate in sessions of the Board of Trustees and attend the trustee committee meetings. They are not, of course, voting members of this body but they are permitted to speak, to take part in discussions, and even to bring recommendations to the Board.

At Findlay College in Ohio a student is placed on the four standing committees of the Board of Trustees as an advisory member. The annual spring meeting of the Board of Trustees at Claremont Men's College in California is a two-day affair held on campus. Students, faculty, and alumni attend all except one business session and discussion involves those questions which seem to be most pressing and important at that time.

Regis College in Colorado had an interesting experience in regard to student participation on the Board of Trustees. The Student Executive Board—seven students elected by the student body—requested the president of the college, in the late spring of 1967, to permit student representation with voting privileges on all faculty committees, beginning in the fall of 1967. It was evident from conversations of the Student Executive Board with the president of Regis College that the board did not know the function, operation, responsibility, or authority of the standing faculty committees. After some time in which the seven students reassessed their request, the Student Executive Board requested voting representation on the following committees: Board of Trustees, President's Council, and the Faculty Committees on Educational Policies, Student Life, Admissions and Degrees, Student Health, Athletics, Lecturers, Library, Faculty and Institutional Research, and Student Advising and Counseling. It should be noted that the Student Executive Board did not request voting representation, in fact no membership whatsoever, on the Faculty Committee on Rank and Tenure and the Faculty Committee on Student Aid and Scholarships.

The president of the college referred the matter to the Board of Trustees for judgment in its own case, and to the faculty members of his committee. There was unanimity that (1) the faculty committee members would welcome a student representative, and (2) the student representative should be a nonvoting participant at least for one year. The Board of Trustees denied the request for student membership or representation, but determined to invite the president of the Student Executive Board to attend "an occasional meeting of the Board of Trustees." The President's Council followed the example of the Board of Trustees.

Selection of student representatives was made by each faculty committee from among the seven members of the elected Student Executive Board, and appointments were announced in June 1967. The president indicated that "we are optimistic and have reason to expect this will be a worthwhile and respected innovation for Regis College government."

Mary Hardin-Baylor College in Texas has a student representative sit with the college's Board of Governors and Trustees at general meetings and the student can enter into discussions. Major committees of the Board of Trustees have student representatives. Finally, Rockhurst College in Missouri has the president of the student council as an ex-officio member of the Board of Regents. The Board of Regents is not the legal governing body but an advisory board which does, however, carry considerable weight in policy decisions.

STUDENT INVOLVEMENT IN FACULTY EVALUATION

The evaluation of teaching on the college level has received increasing attention in recent years. Faculty members, administrators, and the students themselves have become increasingly interested in and concerned about the quality of teaching in college. Five hundred and forty institutions out of the usable responses, the equivalent of 61.2 per cent, indicated that their students were involved in some form of faculty evaluation. Two hundred and twelve, or 39.3 per cent of the usable responses, indicated they had the practice prior to 1961; 274 institutions, or 50.7 per cent, had the practice in 1961 or later, while 54 institutions, or 10 per cent, stated they were planning to involve students in faculty evaluation. (See Table 4.)

The initiation of teacher-evaluation programs by students is only part of a wider movement that has affected colleges and universities around the country. Publication of student opinions of professors has been used for purposes ranging from political retribution (at Berkeley) to "helping students avoid" areas of weakness in the curriculum (at Yale). The nationwide panorama of such surveys yields evaluations based on random sampling of 20 per cent of the student body, others based on comprehensive polling of most students, and still others formulated by individual members of specific lecture sections. Methods used include the averaging of numerical ratings and the composition of critiques in essay form.

The increase in student desire for control of their affairs, both academic and personal, is generally acknowledged as the primary motivating factor behind student evaluations of faculty classroom performance. Probably the most widely discussed instance of students' asserting their right to have an influential voice in the evaluation of an instructor's teaching ability took place at Yale University in March 1965. At that time, round-the-clock protest marches greeted the decision of the school's tenure committee to deny tenure to Associate Professor Richard J. Bernstein.

There are many ways in which liberal arts colleges assess faculty. Some of these reported are class visits, opinions of colleagues, chairman evaluation, opinion of the dean, research and publication, informally gathered student opinion, and formal student surveys. Responses by administrators of liberal arts colleges indicate that a large majority of the colleges rely on faculty evaluation by students but that the process is entirely voluntary on the faculty member's part and the professor is the only one who sees the results of the evaluation survey unless he wishes to share them with his department head or the dean. There is no pressure to have him do so. A survey conducted by the American Council on Education indicated that 41 per cent of the liberal arts colleges rely to some degree on informally gathered student opinion while only 4 per cent rely partially on formal student surveys.

There are a growing number of liberal arts colleges that are using formal surveys of student attitudes toward a particular course, usually taken at the end of a semester. The data obtained from an objective questionnaire is then used by the teacher and the dean to assist in evaluating the over-all effectiveness of the course within the curriculum. The reported goals of this course evaluation procedure are twofold: to increase the quality and effectiveness of a course by providing the teacher with information concerning student attitudes toward the course; and to provide information for educational improvements on the administration level. Course evaluation is not without historical precedent. During the Middle Ages when the universities began to be established separate from the monasteries, student recommendations concerning courses were considered an essential aspect of the educational process itself. Teaching was considered a two-way process with both students and teachers bringing to the course whatever each could offer. In more recent times, published course evaluation programs have become solidly established on numerous campuses. Harvard College and Washington State University have had such programs for over forty years. In the early sixties such efforts were copied and became a definite trend on campuses, with questionnaires thoughtfully and carefully prepared. The "Course Critique" published by the *Yale Daily Record,* student newspaper, is an example of the published course evaluation program. The Yale production discusses the nature of each course, the requirements (reading, papers, and the like), and the classroom "style" of each professor. The Harvard pamphlet adds faculty opinions of their own courses.

Emory College in Georgia has an evaluation system which is worth reporting because of the discussions that took place surrounding the implementation of the practice. The basis of the Emory evaluation system is a numerical "grading" scale. Students are asked to give ratings of one (poor) to five (excellent) on a teacher's performance in a certain course. The fifteen categories used are:

1. Organization of course (ex.—was there an outline and did he follow it coherently)
2. Knowledge of subject (ability to answer most questions)
3. Presentation of subject matter (enthusiasm, interest)
4. Preparation for class time (prepared lecture maintaining focus and control)
5. Stimulates interest and creative thought (challenges students to think for themselves; stimulates curiosity in subject matter)
6. Encourages class discussion (allows time for questions, poses questions for discussion)
7. Tolerance of other people's opinions (doesn't impose own point of view, accepts possibility of alternatives)
8. Fair and impartial grading policies (tests graded on merit, grades not influenced by personalities)
9. Interest in student as an individual
10. Value of outside reading (circle O if no outside reading)
11. Value of assigned text (circle O if no text)
12. Value of discussion periods (circle O if no such periods)
13. Class time well spent
14. General estimate of teacher
15. Value of course toward over-all education [5]

All the ratings of a certain teacher for a certain course are averaged for each item by a College Council member.

A number of Emory persons interviewed feel that some explanatory information about courses or professors should be included in the Emory

[5] "Course and Teacher Evaluation." Mimeographed report representing the results of the evaluation of courses and teachers for fall and winter quarters of the school year 1965–66, as compiled by the Faculty Evaluation Committee of the College Council.

survey as well. For example, Dr. Richard F. Starr of the political science department suggests that "the best students" be drafted to write evaluations of courses in essay form, along with passages elucidating the meaning of the statistics and the nature of each course treated. Starr and several other faculty members consider the numerical average dangerous, since, for example, "one student who may have failed the course" in a small class can pull the rating down significantly. Dr. Lyle Downing, also of the political science department, proposes that the number of students giving a certain rating (1, 2, 3, 4, or 5) be presented in the reports rather than an average, since "the average doesn't show how the minority can drag the ratings down."

Dr. Ivor LeClerc of the philosophy department objects to the entire concept of students rating their professors. He maintains that generally the more intelligent minority in a class is weighted down by the majority of duller students, and that students' judgments of a course they have just taken are too likely to be subjective. In his opinion, undergraduates may misunderstand the faculty's methods of conducting a given course, and are not qualified to act as arbiters in the question of professorial ability.

The opposite view is taken by Dr. William Crelly, chairman of the history of art department, who does not feel that the evaluation "generally discourages interested students." The dean of the college calls the information provided by the project "helpful if not taken as the only evidence and determinant" in the matter of faculty ability."[6]

At Stonehill College, Massachusetts, the subject of student involvement in faculty evaluation was first raised by the faculty Rank and Tenure Committee at its meeting in the spring of 1967. The committee believed it desirable to draw up a set of criteria on which the performance of faculty members could be evaluated. Further, it was decided to attach a numerical weight to the various criteria to indicate the degree of importance that the committee attached to each.

After the committee had reached agreement on the criteria and weights, the next problem was the manner in which information concerning a faculty member's rating on these criteria could be obtained. The committee was not satisfied with the present hit-or-miss system of judging one another on "general impression" only. An analysis of the criteria by the committee showed that several sources must be consulted to obtain adequate data on which to base a judgment.

The members of the committee reasoned that, first, the faculty mem-

[6] Information regarding Emory's course evaluation project and faculty comments taken from Robert Rohrer and Richard Wertheim, "In Spite of Brickbats and Bugs," *Emory College Today*, Summer 1967, pp. 20–22, 42.

ber himself can supply most of the information on his relations outside the college. The various officers of administration know about each one's cooperation in institutional affairs. Particularly the department chairman is in a position to supply information on this subject as well as the general competence of the members of his department. This left one final source of information, the students. "Being teachers," said the chairman of the Rank and Tenure Committee, "the members of the Committee were well aware of the inadequacies of student rating sheets. But, we were forced to the position that some sort of student survey is desirable."

According to the academic dean of Stonehill College, the reasons for the decision on the necessity of student opinion are as follows:

1. Students are, in fact, already reporting their opinions of classes to administrators and faculty members. All of us are forming impressions of our colleagues from these reports. Often, these criticisms emanate from a small, but vocal, minority of the students. It seems necessary, for the teacher's protection, that some way be found to allow all the students in a class to be heard.

2. A survey conducted several years ago showed that 40 per cent of American colleges already use student surveys. Our students have approached me several times this year to get my blessing on their conducting such a survey and publishing the results. Our best way to forestall irresponsible surveys is to conduct a responsible one ourselves.

3. Positive benefits can come from student ratings, apart from the gathering of the information desired by the Committee. It helps encourage the student to reflect on the course and its objectives; it gives the student the feeling that he is sharing in the course and so creates a better spirit of cooperation between faculty and student; and it provides feedback to the teacher on how the students perceive him and the course.

4. With more and more student election coming into the curriculum, it is increasingly important that faculty members be aware of how students view them, so that they can guard against developing antagonisms.

The idea of student evaluation was met with mixed reactions at Stonehill. About half the faculty used a student survey form on an experimental basis at the end of the spring semester. The form went directly from student to teacher. At a faculty meeting held in November 1967, the faculty was asked to vote on whether the forms should be mandatory in all classes and whether they should be reviewed not only by the teacher but by the dean and the department chairman as well. The vote was 39 yes, 11 no.

Other colleges that use extensive published course and faculty evaluation programs are the College of Arts and Letters of the University of Notre Dame, the Liberal Arts College of the University of Arizona, the School of Liberal Arts of the University of Pittsburgh, Grand Valley State

College in Michigan, McMicken College of Arts and Sciences of the University of Cincinnati, the College of Arts and Sciences of the University of Washington, Bates College in Maine, and San Diego State College. At San Diego State College, faculty evaluation by students has been going on for three years through *The Faculty Register*. This eighty-page document gives student ratings of faculty members as to value of a course, effectiveness of the professor, tests, and other items. For two years it was sold off campus, but last year it was distributed at the book store. In autumn of 1965, the first volume of *Course Critique* was published by the Associated Students of the University of Washington. *Course Critique* was financed from the student activity budget and was prepared and edited by students. Student opinion of 175 elected lower-division courses was compiled from 6,000 completed questionnaires distributed to students through the student newspaper in the spring of 1965. A second and "improved" *Course Critique* was published in the autumn of 1966—again, with student funds and student preparation and editing. This 270-page book rated approximately 800 courses and faculty on the basis of approximately 24,000 questionnaires returned by students to whom they were mailed. It was generally agreed that the second *Course Critique* was an improvement over the first in objectivity and accuracy; however, the faculty generally feel that the objectives of the *Course Critiques* can be achieved in other ways.

The students of the Liberal Arts College at Notre Dame have produced a listing that reports the courses, the readings involved, the number and kind of papers, and the mode of presentation used by the professor. Critical evaluation enters into this listing by excluding courses and professors not deemed worthwhile in the student consensus. The dean of the college encourages cooperation by department chairmen and professors but makes it clear that he is not sponsoring the project nor financing it.

There are some colleges who reported that student opinion is sampled in making faculty tenure decisions. At Westmont College in California, for example, no faculty member is given tenure without some sampling of student opinion through questionnaires. Until about two years ago, the dean could ask the students to evaluate a faculty member only with his permission, but since that time the entire faculty has voted to give the dean permission to evaluate any or all their classes in any given quarter and to get some over-all rating of their performance through the student evaluation of the total academic program. In 1965 the dean of faculty made a trial run, with an improvised questionnaire, trying to evaluate student response to the total academic program. It was so well received and seemed so valuable that a committee devised a questionnaire of thirty-five parts which was administered to over 500 students out of a student body of 650. The information gleaned from this student evaluation is now being studied at faculty meetings and in various committees. A course which had been required for graduation for many years was dropped from the requirements on the basis of the student questionnaire. Some of Westmont's part-time teachers and one or two of the temporary teachers were dismissed, partly because of their poor rating by students on the questionnaire.

"One of our faculty members," said the dean of Westmont College, "who now has tenure almost certainly would not have been granted such had we used this device a few years ago. I would have one word of caution for anyone who would begin to use these questionnaires. Students expect to see results!"

Western Maryland College is another institution that uses student opinion in making tenure determinations. The college has a pattern of one-year faculty appointments, three-year appointments, and then tenure. The second of these appointments seems to be the trouble spot and the dean, who makes recommendations to the Administrative Advisory Council in January whether or not to offer the three-year appointment, supplements the department head's opinion with a generous sampling of the opinions of "responsible" students. "These contributions have proved so valuable," says the dean, "that I plan this year to ask the student government for a Dean's Cooperative Committee, which will gather and present student opinion to assist in these and other decisions of a similar nature."

At Earlham College in Indiana, faculty evaluation by students for administrative purposes, that is, for decisions concerning tenure, promotion, salary increases, is carried on rather informally. The informality does not mean that student evaluation of faculty lacks significance and influence. When the administration discusses with the Faculty Affairs Committee a question of promotion or tenure, members of the committee, as well as the chairman of the department involved and the dean of the college, actively seek comprehensive student evaluation about the person in question.

Another approach to the involvement of students in faculty evaluation is the personal approach. At Muskingum College in Ohio, juniors and seniors play a predominant role in selecting two distinguished teachers each year. In addition, each year, the academic dean meets with ten seniors selected from each academic department to evaluate the faculty in that department. "I personally believe," says the academic dean at Muskingum, "that students are better judges of effective professors than the professors' peers. I prefer seniors to underclassmen for this purpose because their judgment is more mature and their perspective broader."

Individual conferences between the dean of the college and graduating seniors are held at Eastern Mennonite College in Virginia. A less formal procedure is followed at Central College in Iowa where the dean of the college employs a systematic discussion with a cross section of students. These sessions with an invited group take place in the dining hall. The results of the conversations have been found to be equally as reliable as the use of questionnaires.

At Williams College in Massachusetts, each year the president invites all members of the graduating class, grouped according to major subject, to meet with him and asks general questions about their educational experience at Williams College. He does not ask their opinions about specific teachers or courses; rather, he asks them to discuss which courses and insights they regard as being most valuable.

STUDENT INVOLVEMENT IN FACULTY SELECTION

While students are involved on faculty committees and in faculty evaluation, most colleges draw the line when it comes to including students in the faculty selection process. However, 23 colleges or 2.6 per cent of the total usable response, did indicate that they had a procedure for including students in the selection of faculty. (See Table 4.)

The academic dean at Jamestown College in North Dakota expressed surprise that few institutions involve students in the selection of faculty. "I began this practice last year," said Dean Dale J. Shaw, "and found it to be extremely helpful and I assumed that it was probably fairly widespread." Faculty candidates are required to visit the campus at the college's expense prior to their employment. While at Jamestown, they meet with upperclassmen majoring in the area for which the candidate is being considered. The student body is small enough to permit the college to invite every upperclassman within the given major. The candidate is introduced and his education and experience are summarized. A dialogue then begins between the students and the candidate which lasts for about an hour. The faculty and administrative staff may also attend but the primary interaction is between the candidate and the students. Following the interview, and before a decision is made, the students are asked to give their opinion. Dean Shaw explained:

I find this more valuable by far than the customary interview techniques. One learns a great deal about a man by watching him thinking on his feet and fielding questions that are often barbed and difficult to answer. So far, we have had student approval on all candidates but this covers only about five people. Four of these were hired and one was not. I don't really know what our reaction would be if we were to want a man and the students turned thumbs down. However, I suspect that it would strongly mitigate against our hiring him. Perhaps the future will pose such a problem.

At Chatham College, Pennsylvania, when a person is being considered as a candidate for a position he is brought to the campus for at least a day, longer if possible. The program for the day is planned so that he meets with members of the department for which he is being considered and with other faculty members. Arrangements are made for the candidate to have lunch with a group of students, usually majors in his field. If it is impossible for students to lunch with the candidate they meet him informally over coffee. Everyone who meets the candidate submits his opinion of the candidate's suitability for the position either in writing or orally. These opinions are all transmitted to the president and the dean who are the last ones to meet the candidate. Student opinion is considered a vital part of this process. President Eddy's assistant said:

I can recall at least two instances where faculty members were favorably impressed by a candidate but the students were not and the candidate was not hired. We feel that the judgment of the students is extremely important in evaluating future faculty members. We also feel that the prospective faculty member should have an opportunity to see the kind of student he will be teaching.

The same types of procedures exist at Gettysburg College in Pennsylvania, Union College in Kentucky, and Albion College in Michigan. At Earlham College in Indiana students interview each prospective faculty member and give the administration their judgment of his potential. No faculty members or administrators are around during this interview, which often goes on over dinner and following it. Students who do the interviewing are picked at random and consist of majors from the prospective faculty member's department and others from the general student body. Sometimes they are picked by the dean, sometimes they are picked by the department chairman, sometimes one student is asked to get together an appropriate group to interview a particular person. The students' reactions and suggestions are considered by the administration and by the Faculty Affairs Committee in making a decision about the prospect.

At Raymond College of the University of the Pacific in California, students' views in the evaluation of potential new faculty members are earnestly solicited and respected. The provost reports that "we would not bring into the college a teacher to whom student reaction is negative. Students were given this right to dissent even in the choice of the provost."

Tusculum College, Tennessee, is another institution which involves students in faculty selection. This takes place at the time of the faculty prospect's visit to the campus for an interview. The professor is introduced to a selected, small group of students who are majoring in that discipline and left alone with those students for a period of time. It is conveyed to the individuals involved that this is an opportunity to get acquainted with the caliber of the other. It also serves to demonstrate the kind of respect for students inherent in the philosophy and practice at Tusculum. After the visit, the students report their impressions in writing or orally to President Douglas G. Trout who stated:

Students welcome this opportunity and respond to it with amazing maturity and responsibility. I know of no instance in which students' views were contrary to assessments already made, but they have confirmed some borderline cases which subsequently were rejected as faculty candidates here. Perhaps the most delightful experience in this connection was the series of involvements in the selection of a Dean of Women. The result is that we bypassed trained and experienced "student personnel workers" and contracted a profoundly wise, married (with two teen-age children) woman who has "only" a Michigan B.A. in anthropology as her academic background. She is the finest Dean of Women I have seen.

SUMMARY

An examination of liberal arts college activities in the area of student participation in governance leads to the conclusion that more and more colleges are searching for methods of student involvement. Even colleges which do not actually involve students in the decision-making process at the present time are aware that they are going to have to think about this matter and do something positive in the direction of student involvement. At the University of Alaska, for instance, the dean of students writes "I believe we are currently in a transition phase from student government being concerned only with administering their own programs to real participation in the governance of the University." The vice president for administration at Whitman College in Washington has no doubt as to the general direction in which student opinion is progressing. "They wish to be represented on every committee," he states, "even though the activity of that committee might be clearly out of their own area of activity and possible responsibility." At Drew University in New Jersey a new committee, composed of faculty and students, in the fall of 1968 launched a thorough study of student life. In the fall of 1967 studies and discussions, intended to bring students more directly into several areas of policy making, took place at Frostburg State College in Maryland, St. John's University College of Arts and Sciences in Minnesota, Tufts University College of Liberal Arts in Massachusetts, and St. Cloud State College in Minnesota.

Evaluative statements in regard to student participation in institutional direction have been quite favorable in those institutions where students have had a role to play. The dean of instruction at Sonoma State College in California says:

It is my very strong feeling that the great majority of the faculty at Sonoma State College cherishes the idea of close relationships with the students. The smallness of the college at the present time has fostered this ideal. As we grow larger many of the faculty are concerned that this feeling of closeness may disappear. Therefore, I think that our attempt to involve students as we have is not only a recognition of the contributions that they can make to the well-being of the college but is also an attempt on the part of the faculty to maintain a governing framework which fosters the idea of close relationships with the students.

At Chico State College in California, the dean of administration writes:

You might be interested to know that in this past year student participation in college policy, discussions, and decisions has been extremely mature, has been very well received by students and faculty alike, has resulted in a better relationship by the students and the administration and the faculty, and has, as a whole, been a completely satisfactory operation in all respects.

There is another trend developing which allows students to have contact with the administration rather than serving on faculty committees. For example, at Barry College a "President's Dialogue" has been formalized. The president meets with students in groups of twenty-five, once a month, and discusses various topics of interest, from school regulations to plans for the growth of the college. The students usually determine the topics of discussion. At Adams State College in Colorado, a President's Advisory Committee, made up entirely of students, meets with the president of the college for purposes of interchange of ideas. A President's Academy was organized in 1965 by the president of Fairfield University in Connecticut. Membership is open to any undergraduates who apply in writing and agree to attend monthly meetings. During the monthly meetings, university problems are discussed. Southern Oregon College has weekly luncheons involving the president of the college, the president of the Student Senate and the president of the Faculty Senate. This is called the Triad Club and a great many matters involving student views in regard to institutional direction are discussed.

The vice president and dean of the college of Ripon College in Wisconsin sums up the role of student involvement on committees as follows:

There was a vocal minority of faculty members opposed to student membership on the Curriculum Committee. The arguments were the usual ones that the students lacked the necessary maturity of judgment and experience, that the Faculty was paid to run the curriculum, that the administration was abdicating its responsibilities in the running of the College, and so forth *ad nauseam*. My experience with student representation on faculty committees leads me to believe that they can be extremely valuable in bringing a point of view as well as a kind of knowledge and experience which adult members of the College community simply do not possess.

STUDENT SERVICES

ADMISSIONS

Despite the fact that a good number of liberal arts colleges indicated in response to the questionnaire that they had unique admissions practices, the admission of students in the majority of colleges in the country is still based on high school grades and scores on standardized tests such as College Boards or the ACT.

One of the variations in admissions that is being considered by a growing number of liberal arts colleges is related to attempts to deal with "disadvantaged" students in special ways. For example, at Trinity College in Connecticut, the college is granting admittance to men who would not ordinarily be able to meet Trinity's requirements successfully and is starting them in reduced load programs, often accompanied by student tutoring. Greenville College in Illinois for the past few years has been conducting a precollege session to give students with weak high school background a chance to qualify for college admission. Originally, these students were invited to attend the summer session before college, but recently the policy has been modified and now the students start in the fall with the other regularly admitted freshmen. A special tutor program is provided to assist these students to qualify for regular admission in the second semester of the freshman year. The special group of students all take the same courses, limited to twelve semester hours, and each one has a special student tutor assigned in each course that he is taking.

The variations in admissions practices at San Francisco State College are mainly in the area of disadvantaged students. In the last two years the college has made special efforts to bring minority and disadvantaged students who have college potential into the freshman class and into special programs. Specifically, they have worked with a group on campus called the Black Students Union and in the fall of 1967–68 admitted over forty Negro students identified by the Union and tested by the staff of San Francisco State. They have also brought in a number of students from the Sausalito Teacher Education Program (STEP) who are representatives of minority groups striving to be teachers (fifteen students).

One other program, Upward Bound, has been allowed to sponsor about ten students under special admission practices.

Dunbarton College of Holy Cross in Washington, D.C., makes some exceptions in admissions requirements in favor of applicants from inner city schools. Fort Lewis College, Colorado, admits a small number of marginal students as unclassified students for the eight-week session during the last portion of the spring trimester. The students take from six to eight hours of regular college courses with the understanding that their success or failure in these courses will directly affect the final decision concerning their application for admission to the fall trimester as regular students. The dean of the college at the College of Arts and Sciences of Florida State University has the option of waiving the admission requirements and recommending admission for students who might be otherwise inadmissible. In addition, the State Board of Regents has authorized the college to admit, to 5 per cent of the freshman class, students who would not otherwise be academically eligible. This has led the college into a program for the identification of disadvantaged students through the Upward Bound Program and to make a search to diversify the freshman class with students of low socioeconomic status or those who, according to the dean, "would normally be considered poor bets for admission."

Tusculum College in Tennessee is representative of a growing number of colleges that are using their summer session to assist high school graduates in overcoming deficiencies. Tusculum accepts some students conditionally on their attendance at a no-credit Summer Institute in Basic Skills held on campus in August. The institute consists of remedial course work in English Grammar and Composition, Mathematical Reasoning, and Reading and Study Skills. At the end of the institute, achievement tests in mathematics and English are administered. Students making high scores on these tests may apply for a waiver of the freshman requirement in English 101 and Beginning Mathematics.

Although Grand Canyon College in Arizona uses rank in high school as the primary basis for admission, it gives some consideration to the number and type of extracurricular activities in which a student has been involved. Thus a student who may be a marginal risk academically may be admitted if he has been very active in music, drama, journalism, or the like. Such students are given provisional admission.

At the other end of the spectrum, there are some practices which colleges have designed to vary their admissions for gifted students. A number of gifted freshmen at Trinity College, Connecticut, are allowed to by-pass any or all basic requirements so that they may enter courses in which they have special interests. In addition, these same students may engage in special projects independent of or in conjunction with members of the faculty. At Cornell College in Iowa a few exceptional high school students, who show by outstanding achievement and performance on examinations that they are prepared to carry a program of study toward a college degree, may be accepted for admission and permitted to enroll before graduation from high school. The college has had the program for about ten years and annually admits one or two students through the program. The dean of Cornell College indicated that this has been a successful program and most of the students who had been accepted have completed their college degree within the regular four years.

Several departments such as the department of foreign languages and classics and the department of history of the College of Arts and Sciences at the University of Maine administer achievement tests to their entering freshmen. Freshmen who achieve certain established scores are exempt from introductory courses and are allowed to move directly into more advanced work. No degree credit is given, however, for the by-passed introductory courses.

At Plymouth State College in New Hampshire the program of early identification of the gifted is carried on in very close cooperation with the guidance counselors in the state through the New Hampshire Personnel and Guidance Association. Counselors throughout the state keep the college informed of gifted students in their secondary school systems. In addition, during the orientation period at the beginning of the fall semester, locally constructed proficiency examinations are administered to all students in science, mathematics, business education, foreign language, and English. As a result of these examinations, some basic courses may be waived and the student is permitted to register for more advanced courses.

The importance of accommodating the individual differences of young people of similar age is widely recognized, yet many of our conventional academic arrangements inhibit the nurturing of these individual talents and capacities. Over the years we have developed the "grade system" as a convenient administrative device for handling the traffic management problems of our schools. Each child begins at age six and moves forward "one grade each year until he emerges from high school twelve years later. Then he may march through four years of college, still in step with his chronological peers."[7] This solution to the problem of educational logistics has many administrative advantages, but pressed toward its logical extreme it defeats our efforts to serve the individual capacities of children.

[7] From *They Went to College Early,* A Report on the Early Admission to College Programs of Education (New York: Fund for the Advancement of Education, 1957) p. vi.

At its worst it has become a chronological lock-step which in practice, if not in theory, treats students of similar age as if they were all alike instead of all different. The most serious victims—the most handicapped students under the lock-step arrangement—turn out to be our ablest youngsters for whom the pace is too slow and the academic diet too thin.[8]

The Program for Early Admission at Elizabethtown College in Pennsylvania represents one possible approach to making colleges more flexible and more effective in developing the diversified abilities of young people. The student who at the end of his junior year in high school qualifies for admission through this program is selected on the basis of specific criteria. He is absorbed into the regular college program as a freshman taking the regular courses that all freshman students take as part of any prescribed degree curriculum. Students are selected for the program on the basis of regular application subject to the following general criteria:

1.   High academic achievement as indicated by their high school records
2.   Must have completed the eleventh grade of an accredited high school program
3.   Test scores are considered
4.   Mature appearance is considered
5.   Rating scores by teachers and counselors involving such areas as a sense of responsibility, emotional stability, self-reliance, adaptability, high motivation for college, and social maturity
6.   Evidence of sound ability in interpersonal relations and freedom from excessive parental pressure toward early admission

The following individuals participate in the selecting process:

1.   The director of admissions of Elizabethtown College
2.   The dean of instruction
3.   College department heads
4.   The principal of the applicant's high school
5.   The guidance counselor of the applicant's high school
6.   The director of testing of Elizabethtown College

McNeese State College, Louisiana, initiated a program of early admission beginning with the 1963 summer session. This program is open to academically superior high school juniors. The purpose of the program is to attempt to meet the educational needs of the more able students through enrichment as well as controlled acceleration. A candidate for this program must have a cumulative grade-point average of 3.0 or better

[8] *They Went to College Early, op. cit.,* pp. vi–vii.

on all work taken in high school and must have the recommendation of his principal. Students recommended are invited to the McNeese campus to take a series of college entrance tests for further screening, and for possible future use in placement and guidance. Students selected are enrolled in regular freshman college classes, and receive deferred credit at McNeese State College on completion of the summer term. This credit becomes a part of his college permanent record when the student graduates from high school and furnishes the McNeese registrar with his completed high school transcript. The transfer of credit to other institutions depends on the policies of that particular institution.

Enrollment in college classes is based on interest and aptitude as assessed by the Testing and Guidance Bureau. A student cannot enroll for more than two courses.

Some colleges have attempted to relieve the pressure of multiple applications. Hanover College in Indiana, Pfeiffer College in North Carolina, and Salem State College in Massachusetts, and others have a pattern of "rolling" admissions where there is no one date on which the college notifies all applicants of their acceptance. Instead, candidates are notified of acceptance on a continuing basis over a period of time. At Salem State, acceptance notification starts about January 15 and continues over a period of several months. The member colleges of the Associated Colleges of the Midwest (ACM)[9] offer candidates for admission the opportunity to apply for admission by means of a single application method. The candidate interested in being considered by two or more ACM colleges files only one application, his secondary school provides only one copy of his high school transcript and record form, and he pays only one application fee of $15.00. If the candidate is accepted by the college that is his first choice, his application is not considered by the other colleges on his list. If he is not accepted by his first-choice college, his application papers are forwarded by that college to the admissions office of his first alternate college. If he is accepted by this college, he is not considered by the other colleges he has listed. If he is not accepted by his first alternate choice, his application papers are forwarded to the college he has placed next on his list. This process is continued until the candidate has been accepted by a college he has listed or has been considered by all of the colleges on his list.

[9] The colleges that are members of the Associated Colleges of the Midwest are: Beloit College, Wisconsin; Carleton College, Minnesota; Coe College, Iowa; Cornell College, Iowa; Grinnell College, Iowa; Knox College, Illinois; Lawrence University, Wisconsin; Monmouth College, Illinois; Ripon College, Wisconsin; St. Olaf College, Minnesota.

Finally, a six-semester admission policy was adopted in 1968 for a two-year trial period by four-year colleges in the state of Washington. Under this new policy, admission will be based on six semester high school records, instead of the seven previously required. According to J. Robert Long, director of High School Relations and associate director of admissions for the University of Washington, this early application date "will speed up the admission process considerably. In essence, it will allow a student to apply earlier and receive information concerning his acceptance sooner than it was possible in the past." It is not compulsory and a student may apply earlier only if he wishes to.

ADVANCED PLACEMENT

The Advanced Placement Program of the College Entrance Examination Board, briefly stated, is a program in which secondary schools offer work believed to be at the college level and the Educational Testing Service supervises the administration of college-level final examinations. Colleges, on the basis of data made available by the program, may then grant to candidates placement in an advanced section of a subject, or credit hours toward graduation, or both placement and credit.

Returns from the questionnaire indicate that 708 (80.2 per cent) of the 882 responses have an advanced placement program. Of the 708 colleges, 305 (43.1 per cent) introduced the practice prior to 1961; 370 (52.2 per cent) introduced the practice in 1961 or after; 33 (4.7 per cent) are planning to introduce an advanced placement program. (See Table 4.)

Many American colleges have recognized the considerable difference in the level of achievement already attained by their entering students. The practice of granting placement in an advanced section, credit toward graduation, or both placement and credit in recognition of college-level work completed prior to entrance to college is very old indeed. Alexander Hamilton, for example, after one year of preparation at a grammar school in Elizabeth, New Jersey, applied for admission with advanced status at Princeton. When turned down, ambitious young Hamilton made similar application to King's College in New York where he was accepted with the advanced status that he sought. Another well-known example is Horace Mann, who in the early nineteenth century was admitted with sophomore standing to Brown University after relatively little preparatory schooling. Individual examples of advanced placement continued to occur throughout the nineteenth and twentieth centuries. However, prior to the Advanced Placement Program of the College Entrance Examination Board, awards of such placement and credit were exceptional and entirely dependent on local standards, never part of a clearly defined and nationwide program.

One of the experiments in advanced placement was that begun at the University of Buffalo in 1932. The university granted credit and placement to students who performed satisfactorily on three-hour examinations comparable to final examinations for college courses. Through operation of the plan over a period of decades, and through evaluative studies, the University of Buffalo contributed much evidence in support of granting such credit. The program of College Credit Examinations at Buffalo was intended to accomplish three objectives: (1) achieve better articulation between schools and the University of Buffalo; (2) provide a more appropriate educational pattern and increased stimulus for independent study on the part of high-ability students; and (3) attract able students to the university.[10]

The University of Connecticut began in 1955–56 an even more ambitious plan than that of the University of Buffalo. Beginning the first year with 108 able high school students, over four times that number were involved a decade later. Under its Cooperative Program for Superior Students the university approves of schools, teachers, and students deemed qualified to participate in college-level study. Teachers are provided with items such as syllabi, reading lists, and examinations in order to teach approved college courses to able seniors. Those students passing with *C* or better are awarded college credit by the registrar of the university.

Shortly after World War II national needs and international problems caused renewed attention to be given not only to the goals and the quality of education in general, but more immediately to the possibility of making more efficient the education of unusually able and ambitious students.[11] It was in this postwar, cold war, milieu that the Fund for the Advancement of Education supported four major studies intended to shed light on the teaching of the academically able. One, the Portland study, was intended to examine ways in which a whole school system, top to bottom, could improve the education of the gifted. Another, the Early Admissions experiment, enticed youngsters into leaving high school at the end of the sophomore or junior year in order to matriculate as college freshmen. The third study underwritten by the Fund resulted in a recommendation that the College Board establish a program of advanced placement as a means of

[10] W. L. Barnette, "Advanced Credit for the Superior High School Student," *Journal of Higher Education,* 38, January 1957, 15.

[11] For a history of the Advanced Placement Program see Donald Bruce Elwell, "A History of the Advanced Placement Program of the College Entrance Examination Board to 1965." Unpublished Ed.D. dissertation, Teachers College, Columbia University, 1967.

improving articulation and encouraging a more rigorous program of studies in secondary school. The fourth study, the School and College Study of Admission with Advanced Standing, was based on faith in the ability of secondary schools and colleges to work together to test two premises: (1) that some gifted students can proficiently do college-level work while still in secondary school, and (2) that some secondary school teachers can effectively teach the college material. The program proved to be successful and in October 1954 the College Entrance Examination Board agreed to assume responsibility for the continuation and expansion of the program. The first examination under its sponsorship was administered in May 1956. By 1960 it was generally acknowledged that the Advanced Placement Program of the College Board had succeeded in retaining the essential features of the School and College Study while transforming it into a program of national dimensions.

Advanced placement has within it elements of both enrichment and acceleration. Charles R. Keller's "iceberg theory" of the Advanced Placement Program implies that the visible operations of the program are small compared to the "hard-to-measure intangibles and by-products."

It has been one of the most important educational catalysts during the past decade. . . . It has affected curricular thinking, course planning, and teaching. It has improved communication between schools and colleges. . . . It has raised the intellectual tone in both schools and colleges.[12]

The bulk of the iceberg is still not visible, but it is possible to note the direction in which it is moving.

One development that can be expected is continued growth in the number of talented students identified and channeled into advanced courses. Already in existence at Harvard, and perhaps coming soon to more colleges, is a kind of two-track college option in which the student is given considerable flexibility in the light of different levels of preparation in secondary schools. Students of average ability or from mediocre schools will generally require the usual four-year college curriculum, but a considerable number of students will reduce the time spent in college by one year by means of advanced placement.

[12] Charles R. Keller, "The Advanced Placement Program: An Educational Catalyst" (1966), pp. 3–4. (Mimeographed.)

Chapter 5

REORGANIZATION AND RESTRUCTURING OF THE LIBERAL ARTS COLLEGE

DESPITE THE GROWING EMPHASIS ON THE IMPORTANCE OF THE HUMAN element in the teaching-learning process, the environment in which learning takes place is receiving increasing attention in higher education. While everyone can agree that the quality of the teacher who sits on one end of the log and the nature of the student who sits on the other end are all-important in the learning process, nevertheless the kind of log they sit on can well determine the success of the interrelationships between the teacher, the student, and knowledge. Table 5 gives some indication of the amount of activity that is going on in higher education in campus planning. We have singled out two items for particular attention—the college calendar and the library.

The College Calendar

Revamping academic calendars has been popular among colleges and universities during recent years. (See Table 5.) Educators' parlance has been enriched with such terms as "three-three plan" and "four-one-four." As the information on calendar innovations was processed, it became apparent that the college calendar is just one factor which interacts with others to form the college's over-all program. Usually, desired modifications in some aspect of the college program other than the calendar necessitated a change in the latter. Among the reasons underlying a calendar change were the introduction of a new curriculum, a desire to reduce the time a student must spend in college to graduate, a plan to allow students to spend concentrated periods on a limited number of subjects, and a determination to provide time for off-campus study or for additional independent study. It also became apparent that, as far as calendar changes were concerned, the quarter and trimester systems were of such universality as to place them out of the category of innovative practices.

FIRST SEMESTER ENDS BEFORE CHRISTMAS

This plan accounted for the greatest number of schools among those reporting calendar innovations. The calendar calls for two semesters of traditional length with the first semester beginning in late August or early September and ending before Christmas. The second semester begins the second week in January and runs until the middle or the end of May. A few colleges reported a somewhat longer vacation between semesters—as much as five or six weeks—to give students and faculty members time for travel, research, and, when necessary, job training.

Ripon College, Wisconsin, finishes the first semester before Christmas. To do so they begin classes about September 1, have no extended vacation other than a Thanksgiving weekend during the first semester, have a long Christmas vacation, begin the second semester about January 10, have a two-week spring vacation, and hold Commencement about May 20. The academic dean of Siena Heights College, Michigan, reported that the faculty was eager to adopt a calendar which would provide for completion of the first semester before the Christmas recess. They thought the two or three weeks after the Christmas vacation before the semester examinations were wasted by faculty and students. Salem College, West Virginia, also broke away from tradition by eliminating the lame-duck session after the Christmas holidays. They now complete the fall semester in fifteen weeks before Christmas, have approximately three weeks' vacation before the second semester starts, and then have a second semester of sixteen weeks with a two-weeks spring vacation in the middle of the sixteen-week period. Salem College ends the year around May 18. The plans for changing to their present calendar were studied by the faculty and voted by them. After one year of operation, the dean of the college reports that "the faculty, students, and administration are all pleased with the plan." The dean also indicated that Salem feels that the long spring vacation is necessary because

. . . from our experience that is the restless time of year with students all pent-up and full of excess energy. After the vacation, they come back subdued, settled, and ready to complete the last half of the semester in a much more creditable manner.

TABLE 5 LIBERAL ARTS COLLEGES INVOLVED WITH ORGANIZATIONAL INNOVATIONS

Item	Number of Usable Responses to Item a	Percentage of Usable Responses	Before 1961	Percentage of Responses	1961 and After	Percentage of Responses	Planning to Introduce	Percentage of Responses
Substitutes for traditional calendar:								
Quarter	118	13.4	61	51.7	40	33.9	17	14.4
Trimester	39	4.4	8	20.5	26	66.7	5	12.8
Other	207	23.5	20	9.6	108	52.2	79	38.2
New campus plans	526	59.6	164	31.2	290	55.1	72	13.7
New styles in classrooms	330	37.4	40	12.1	200	60.6	90	27.3
Experimentation in cost planning	145	16.4	22	15.2	88	60.7	35	24.1
New styles in libraries:								
Facilities	360	40.8	55	15.3	198	55.0	107	29.7
Automation	205	23.2	12	5.9	81	39.5	112	54.6
Learning resource center	316	35.8	82	25.9	113	35.8	121	38.3

a The total number of usable responses to the questionnaire was 882.

Spring Hill College, Alabama, in 1964 introduced a calendar that terminated the first semester before the Christmas holidays. The faculty felt that the advantages of the plan were the elimination of the "rump" session of the fall semester, and the more extended Christmas recess provided opportunity for the faculty to complete the grading of papers and examinations, for the registrar to issue grade reports, for the dean to determine academic status and special programs of deficient students, and for the students and faculty to prepare more effectively for the spring semester. Pacific University and Linfield College in Oregon, West Virginia Wesleyan College, Mount Marty College in South Dakota, Windham College in Vermont, McPherson College in Kansas, Kenyon College in Ohio, and dozens of other colleges around the country have adopted the calendar change allowing the college to complete the first semester before Christmas. They all report that the major purpose was to eliminate the lame-duck session because of the general dissatisfaction with the fragmented schedule for the first semester, which included a break at Thanksgiving, a three-week break at Christmas, returning in January for approximately two weeks, semester examinations, and another semester break. Bruce Haywood, provost of Kenyon College, Ohio, indicated that

a group of us had grown weary of the lame-duck session after the Christmas vacation, a brief period of classes when we found it hard to get ourselves and our students back to the level we had risen to before the holiday. Moreover, we found ourselves beginning the second semester weary and dispirited. The fragmentation of the first semester, we grew convinced, was working against our best teaching efforts. . . . At the same time, we had begun to wonder whether it made sense to split certain courses into two parts. . . . We found in the year course a happy answer to both problems.

Kenyon College now begins their first semester directly after Labor Day. Except for a brief break at Thanksgiving, they run through to about December 21. They have a month's vacation, and start the second semester "renewed and invigorated" about the middle of January. There is a two-week vacation in the middle of March and they end their year late in May. Haywood indicated that the faculty considered other possibilities

. . . but we very much like what we have. Morale in the winter months has been much higher since we made this change. Moreover, we are convinced that the year course is a sound, pedagogical device, encouraging students and teachers to get into their study more thoroughly.

Kenyon's provost reported that the faculty is convinced that one grade in, say, Freshman English makes better sense than two. The faculty also believes that there is a considerable advantage to students and teachers remaining together for the year, rather than parting company after the one semester.

Robert P. Ashley, dean of Ripon College, while stressing the advantages of ending the semester before Christmas, also points out some minor disadvantages. Some students and faculty, he indicated, because of summer school and summer jobs, have difficulty getting back in time for the opening of college. In addition, the fact that Ripon starts their second semester in January makes it impossible for January high school graduates to come to Ripon or for students attending colleges on a traditional calendar to transfer. In addition, several colleges reported that they were unable to complete their spring sports schedule. All in all, however, the colleges that have tried this calendar approach think it is successful and intend to continue.

4–1–4 PLAN

A calendar innovation which is growing in importance on college campuses is the 4–1–4 academic calendar. The main features of the 4–1–4 calendar are a school year divided into two terms, resembling conventional semesters, separated by a January interim. During each of the two semesters, students normally take four full course units rather than a multitude of fragmented courses. The length of the January interim varies from a low of three weeks at one college to a high of six weeks at another. During the month of January students engage in many different kinds of academic activities. Individual colleges usually offer more than one option.

At Luther College, Iowa, regular classes are not in session from January 10 through January 28, and the college's 1,700 students study on campus in special research projects, fulfill on-the-job training in other cities, or study abroad. Art students at Luther College travel in Europe, viewing European art collections; language students absorb the theater and culture of the country whose language they are studying; and economics students study the problem of European economic integration in the Benelux countries. At Carroll College, Wisconsin, the faculty selected the 4–1–4 program as best suited "to achieve the objectives of the college as they are understood today." The faculty were convinced that the 4–1–4 offered desired improvements and flexibility in curricular patterns.

The adoption of the 4–1–4 calendar at St. Olaf College, Minnesota, came as a result of faculty interest in a calendar which would permit more independent work on the part of the students in the interim and which would limit the number of courses taken in any regular semester. At Ohio's Bluffton College, during the three and one-half week interim period, students and faculty members devote themselves to a study of one great issue of our time. In the 1967 interterm Bluffton's faculty and student body focused on an interdisciplinary investigation of "The City." Plans for the interterm had been in the making since January 1966 when the faculty, by a nearly unanimous vote, elected to modify the academic year to allow for the 4–1–4 approach. The semesters were shortened from seventeen to fifteen weeks each. Several concerns prompted the Bluffton faculty action. There was a desire to be rid of the January "lame-duck" period. There was a feeling that students were being compartmentalized within academic disciplines. Moreover, students hesitated to do work in fields unrelated to their major area of competence for fear of lowering their grade-point average. There was a belief that the faculty should reaffirm its conviction that knowledge itself is interdisciplinary and that students, by crossing disciplinary lines, might discover values previously unknown to them. The experiment was planned for two consecutive years and was to be followed by a thorough evaluation.

The colleges which employ the 4–1–4 plan offered the following as advantages for this calendar reform:

1.   During the interim students have an opportunity to study a subject in depth or to leave the campus for an educational experience somewhere in the United States or in another part of the world.

2.   A breakdown of academic compartmentalization occurs and students find themselves involved in interdisciplinary exploration.

3.   Faculty members teach fewer courses during the semester since three four-hour courses usually replace four three-hour courses. The interim period frees some faculty members for study, writing, or research.

4.   The interim period allows colleges to have a more flexible schedule and, in addition, eliminates the post-Chistmas tag-end of the first semester.

There were colleges that noted disadvantages:

1.   Students complained that during the interim they had to do more work than they had expected.

2.   The interim increased the administrative burden on the college. Grades had to be processed more often and the registration process was more complicated than under the semester system.

3–3 PLAN

Over twenty-five years ago Goucher College initiated the 3–3 plan and has used it ever since, although Dartmouth is often credited with devising this arrangement. The double three explains that the student attends college for three terms a year and takes three courses each term. Depending on the college, classes meet three or more times a week for sixty or more minutes. Carleton College in Minnesota, one of the schools on this plan, holds seventy-minute classes three times a week.

The 3–3 plan differs most significantly from other calendar plans in that it requires students to take only three courses at any one time. The basic educational premise of this plan is that by concentrating on only three courses at one time instead of four or five, students will do work of higher quality. Moreover, it is felt that the 3–3 promotes independent study and thus places more responsibility for learning on students.

A number of colleges reported academic calendars which closely resemble the 3–3 but have some modification. St. Peter's College in New Jersey, for example, has a 4–4–3 plan consisting of three ten-week trimesters. In two of the trimesters, students take four courses, and in the remaining trimester take only three. The College of Arts and Sciences of the University of Santa Clara in California has three eleven-week terms. Freshmen and sophomores carry four courses each term and juniors and seniors take three. More independent study is expected of upperclass students. Hartwick College in New York operates under a 3–3–plus calendar. The "plus" represents a three-week term in December during which freshmen and sophomores engage in interdisciplinary sessions and juniors and seniors do independent study. In preparation for the interdisciplinary seminars, students and faculty members are given paperbacks to read during the summer preceding the December term. A college calendar somewhat like Hartwick's is the 10–4–10–10 calendar at Maryville College in Tennessee. Students take three courses during each of the ten-week terms. Maryville differs slightly from Hartwick in that the four-week interim period at the former is devoted to a special project involving independent study. Students advance progressively from the freshman to the senior year in the degree of independence permitted them in their interim period projects.

4/3 OPTION

Bates College in Maine and Judson College in Alabama operate under the 4/3 option. The calendar consists of three terms: two slightly reorganized semesters and a short term of seven or eight weeks in length.

The first semester ends before Christmas and the second near the end of April. The short term extends from the beginning of May through most of June. Students at these colleges can choose one of three roads to graduation. Those students who want to graduate in three years must carry sixteen or seventeen semester hours of credit during the semesters and eight hours during the short term.

Students who choose the traditional four-year road omit the short term and have an extra summer month for work or vacation. However, a third option permits four-year students to take courses during the short term at no additional cost in tuition. In the form of electives, these courses can enrich the student's program. Moreover, if the student takes a sufficient number of courses in a specific area he can graduate with a double major.

OTHER CALENDAR PLANS

Hanover College in Indiana has made changes in its curriculum and in its calendar, and terms its present educational endeavor the "Hanover Plan." The academic calendar consists of two fourteen-week semesters, the first semester ending before Christmas, followed by one five-week term. Students take three courses in each of the semesters and one course during the five-week term.

Another calendar plan designed to enable students to complete their college education in three years is the Quinary Plan used by Northwestern College, Minnesota. The school year begins after Labor Day and is divided into five terms of eight weeks each. A term is patterned after an eight-week summer session, with students taking two or three subjects in each term. Nine or ten weeks of the summer are left free.

Students at Beloit College in Wisconsin receive their education under a three-level, nine-term, four-year calendar, which includes two vacation periods and a field term. Acceleration is possible but is not the usual pattern; students can complete their study, including the required field term, in three weeks short of three years. Kalamazoo College in Michigan designed a program which divided the calendar into four eleven-week quarters. During the freshman and sophomore years students spend the three quarters normally reserved for vacation in some form of experiential education. The junior year consists of as many as two quarters of study abroad and two quarters of study in residence on the campus. The senior year includes one quarter of independent study, one quarter for preparing a senior thesis or research project, and two quarters in residence. The three unusual quarters during the freshman and sophomore years are referred to as "quarters out of residence," and involve experiences approved and controlled by the college; opportunities for vocational exploration through off-campus work and travel may be included.

All these programs have one thing in common—they have attempted to adapt changes to specific needs existing on particular campuses. It is safe to predict that the movement toward calendar reorganization, which has shown substantial growth during the past years, will continue to grow. As college enrollments mount, interest in year-round calendars will be shown by more colleges. As colleges introduce curricular change, there will be modification of the calendar. Students will be taking fewer courses at one time and will concentrate their efforts. Students will complete work for their degrees earlier. There is considerable evidence that the more popular calendar adoptions will be the 4–1–4 and the 3–3 plans.

New Styles in Libraries

The data assembled indicated that in the category of administrative practices the thrust of innovative change was toward the adoption of the Library of Congress Classification as against the Dewey Decimal Classification or other systems. Whether this change has any significance at all for the process of teaching and learning in the liberal arts college is questionable. Its greatest potential lies in the economics of cataloging the books and placing them on the shelves. The problem of centralized cataloging and classification has long engaged the interest of librarians. The current trend appears to be directly linked to Part C of Title II of the Higher Education Act of 1965, by which the Federal Government accepted responsibility for the centralized cataloging of scholarly books as part of its support for higher education.[1]

A growing number of libraries are using various media to support the instructional program in the colleges. (See Table 5.) The media include films, slides, and video tape. Academic libraries obviously are responding to the fact that modern technology is producing the record of mankind and communications materials in new forms; and responding to faculties that are recognizing the range of individual differences in young people. But little is empirically known about the extent to which these audio-visual materials help in the teaching-learning process.[2]

[1] John W. Cronin, *et al.* "Centralized Cataloging at the National and International Level," in *Library Services and Resources,* 2:1, Winter 1967, p. 27.

[2] Richard E. Chapin, "Use of Printed and Audio-Visual Materials for Educational Purposes by College and University Student," in Columbia University, School of Library Service, *Conference on the Use of Printed and Audio-Visual Materials for Instructional Purposes,* edited by Maurice F. Tauber and Irlene R. Stephens (New York: Columbia University, 1966), pp. 57–71.

One of the more ubiquitous innovations in the college library could probably be categorized as a tribute to the copying machine industry. Most of the respondent institutions reported libraries equipped with copying machines and a good percentage of those were introduced since 1961. Similarly innovative is the use of the reader-printer. Such equipment is having a profound influence on the role of the library as a distributor of information, but it is introducing new problems of concern with copyright law. The use of other kinds of machinery has grown less rapidly. Less than 12 per cent of the college libraries report the installation of mechanized circulations systems, with most of these being installed since 1961. This kind of equipment promises to expand the capabilities of loan desks to handle larger numbers of borrowers, and to improve record-keeping procedures. As for other elements of technology, it is apparent that the teletypewriter and facsimile transmission are piquing the interest of librarians. An experimental network using these technologies is already in operation in New York State. Five academic libraries in Connecticut are linked in a teletype network with the Connecticut State Library. The major use of this system is to effect interloans and provide book location service.

The computer made no significant appearance on the library scene before 1961. Computers are rarely integral to the library itself; their high cost limits their use by libraries except when they are installed for other institutional uses and, therefore, also are available to the library. The number of institutions which are considering the introduction of computer technology, compared to the number using it, suggests that this is the innovation of the future. Computer technology holds considerable promise for the mechanization of conventional procedures such as circulation control and serial records, for bibliographical control and text access, and for self-instructional programs. Their future use in the library is supported by the growing number of courses on computer technology in library schools, as well as the number of institutes and summer courses for professional librarians and administrators.

What is of interest in regard to the paperback book, nonbook materials, and microfilms, is not the proportion of institutions which are using them but the number which are not. For example, seventy-one institutions reported that they did not use paperbound books. The most recent issue of *Paperbound Books in Print* lists 48,200 titles.[3] Libraries which reported that they did not use paperbound books apparently reject those titles which appear in that form only. The use of miniaturized print ma-

[3] *Paperbound Books in Print,* 13:2, February 1968 (New York: R. R. Bowker Co., 1968).

terials on film will probably become universal as soon as the reading machines are improved.

Responses dealing with physical facilities in the respondent libraries, the carrels and listening facilities, as well as dial access systems, reflect a focus on the individual and individualized study facilities. A most exciting development in regard to individual seating spaces in the library is the large number of institutions reporting that they are planning to introduce electronically equipped carrels. This development has implications for change in pedagogical method as well as a redeployment of teaching staff and suggests a closer linkage between the classroom and the library. Many librarians reported that they are waiting only for new buildings before they introduce "hot" carrels as well as other innovations.

Librarians were not as responsive to the list of special library services as they were to the other categories. Special libraries usually function than is the academic library. College libraries have long been producing in a commercial or industrial setting. Its proponents claim that its services are more closely supportive of the purposes of its parent institution accessions lists and selective bibliographies, at least for faculty use; some have abandoned these services because of their cost. Other special library services have had little impact on the academic library. A number of librarians noted that such services would require increased professional staffs with greater subject specialization and larger resources. Those institutions which report existing table of contents services and selective dissemination of information may be reflecting a capability made possible by the widespread distribution of photocopy equipment.

If any generalization can be drawn from the data it is that the library is in a state of flux—and perhaps the major constant is change. The increasing momentum of change is particularly apparent if one examines some of the literature bearing on the college library associated with liberal arts programs. Guy R. Lyle, the authority on the American college library, recorded the changes that have taken place in the first part of this century. He concluded:

Not until the twentieth century, and for many colleges not until the twenties and thirties of this century, was there any pronounced change in the traditional role of the library as a storehouse of books and the librarian as guardian of these books.[4]

There have been a number of recorded observations which cast fur-

[4] Guy R. Lyle, *The Administration of the College Library,* Third Edition (New York: H. W. Wilson Co., 1961), p. 1.

ther light on the library, from which both the student and professor draw their sustenance. As recently as 1955, Wyman W. Parker described the liberal arts college entirely in terms of its traditional book stock.[5] Joseph N. Whitten, in a 1958 New York University doctoral dissertation, focused on instructional service as an essential component of the liberal arts college library. He believed that librarians had not fully realized the extent to which they may become engaged in instructional procedures. He concluded that they ought to do so, and that their doing so was "a major and necessary support to the teaching process."[6] Wen Chao Chen, professor of political science and librarian at Kalamazoo College, Michigan, urged, in 1960, that the college library abandon its storehouse role and (1) relate its collections more closely to the academic program, (2) teach students learning skills, (3) reduce student demand for faculty time, and (4) assist faculty members in their research activities. Presumably steps taken to accomplish these goals would be innovational.[7] Further, Benjamin F. Smith in a 1964 article in *Improving College and University Teaching,* stated that the college library was handicapped in fulfilling its education mission by the burden of a system of reserve books which, in his opinion, represented an extension of the textbook. He looked to a resolution of this reserve book problem for improvement of the library.[8]

Now the library is trying to respond to the inadequacy of its traditional techniques of administration and record keeping. It is continuing to move from its passive role of the past and is becoming an active instrument in the process of teaching and learning. The major direction appears to be determined by the library's reflection of the impact of both technology and independent study programs, accompanied by the demand for a wider range of instructional support services. The coherence of these factors is evidenced in the new learning centers and learning resource centers, and in the "library-college" movement.

Learning resource centers are bringing to the campus "stored knowledge" in all forms—printed, photographic, and electronic. The conceptu-

[5] W. W. Parker, "Library in the Liberal Arts College," *College & Research Libraries,* 16, April 1955, pp. 177–182.

[6] Joseph N. Whitten, "Relationship of College Instruction to Libraries in 72 Liberal Arts Colleges" (New York: 1958), *Doctoral Dissertation Abstracts,* 19, January 1959, p. 1766.

[7] Wen Chao Chen, "A Sound Library Service for the Small College," *Liberal Education,* 46, May 1960, pp. 233–240.

[8] Benjamin F. Smith, "Book Reserve System," *Improving College and University Teaching,* 12:2, Spring 1964, 83 ff.

alization and administrative structure of the learning center varies; some are integrated with the library, others are managed separately in the same building or in close proximity.[9] Learning resource centers have been growing vigorously in the secondary schools since the American Association of School Librarians has encouraged the school librarian to assume responsibility for such comprehensive materials centers; their development at the college level has been much slower.

The library-college has been variously described. It is concerned with changing the mode of instruction from the classroom lecture arrangement with the library as a supporting agency, to the electronic carrel in the library with the teaching-learning process dependent on the individual and independent efforts of the student. Recent impetus to this "movement" is derived from the publication of the *Library-College Newsletter* which began publication in May 1965; and in the supporting conferences sponsored by the Graduate School of Library Science of the Drexel Institute of Technology. Jamestown College, North Dakota, defined the library-college in its charter: "The purpose of the Library-College is to increase the effectiveness of student learning particularly through the use of library-centered independent study with a bibliographically expert faculty.[10]

[9] California State College, Hayward. *Learning Resources for Colleges and Universities.* Produced by Fred Harcleroad, Principal Investigator of Project No. OE-3-16-025, Educational Media Branch, Office of Education, U.S. Department of Health, Education and Welfare, September 1964.

[10] Louis Shores, Robert Jordan, and John Harvey, *The Library-College* (Philadelphia: Drexel Press, 1966), p. ix.

Chapter 6

IN CONCLUSION

EVENTS OF THE LAST DECADE HAVE FORCED ON EDUCATORS AN ACKNOWL-edgement of the tentativeness of all mere "facts" and an awareness of their short life in the minds of students. Responses have been a new emphasis in the curriculum on "learning to learn" and on the development in students of abilities and habits of continuous learning; and an emphasis on those outcomes which do endure in the learner: methods of inquiry, concepts, principles, processes, and the like. An older ideal of "coverage" in curriculum construction has yielded to a search for "representative" ideas, "constructs" and experiences, and an awareness that "content" chosen, however important in itself, is more important as a vehicle for fostering and developing these more significant and pervasive outcomes.

The search for new curricular approaches has led to a new emphasis and direction for independent study. Programs of independence have usually been reserved for the superior or honors student but in recent years independent study is being employed as an experience common to all students as well as being introduced at the beginning of a student's college career rather than waiting for the senior year. In addition, the new media and technology have been incorporated into the independent study programs with a growing emphasis on individual study stations equipped with video and audio playback facilities. Another innovative development is the growing use of residence halls as learning centers. While the new dormitories have not utilized to the fullest extent all the technology that is available to make them complete learning centers,

131

there is considerable evidence that liberal arts colleges in recent years are doing more and more to make fuller use of the dormitory as a center for learning as well as living. In some instances faculty office space, various teaching spaces, as well as library spaces, are located in the residence hall, while in other instances the new media are being installed to provide individual learning facilities within the dormitory.

To help support the search for new curricular approaches, developments in new media and technology have been utilized to a growing extent. Developments in the use of the computer hold exciting possibilities for higher education. The growth in the use of television, programmed instruction, dial access retrieval systems, and the development of new teaching auditoriums, as well as facilities for the automatic playback of lectures in both audio and video form, all hold significant possibilities for helping liberal arts college faculties improve the teaching-learning process. In addition, the new technology is being used to help colleges cope with the growing number of students seeking admission.

It must be recognized, of course, that machinery, media, and technology are nothing within themselves. A public address system has little effect on how good the speech is; it only makes it possible for more people to hear it. By the same token, educational media and technology neither make bad teaching good nor good teaching bad. Rather, they extend it, enlarge it, make it more flexible, preserve it, and make it more easily available. Whatever media may be employed, then, the emphasis must remain on the teacher as the designer, or developer, and executor of the instructional program which is presented to the student.

A trend that is gaining momentum in liberal arts colleges across the nation is the admission of students to a greater voice on campus in the area of administrative as well as academic issues. Colleges are searching for methods of involving students on important college committees as well as finding means for more meaningful student-faculty and student-administrative contact. The future will see students admitted as a policy-making partner in higher education.

In recent years, there have been a number of new developments in higher education. We have stressed from the very beginning that the developments discussed in the foregoing chapters do not necessarily represent "first ideas" in higher education. If we define innovation as "first ideas" we may have to stop studies of innovation with the Greeks. For example, the idea of what we are now calling "learning-living complexes" was being discussed by Daniel Coit Gilman at Johns Hopkins as early as 1893. Programmed instruction was being discussed as early as 1926; independent study for undergraduates has been under way at least since the 1890's; and even the idea of freshman seminars has celebrated at least eleven birthdays and probably can be traced back into previous decades. What is suggested by our analysis of developments in liberal arts colleges in the nation is that higher education has begun to move, and many ideas have begun to take hold—in new and expanded ways— in a variety of different kinds of institutions. It is very possible that the historians of higher education will refer to the present time as a period of innovation in education as well as the time for making available the benefits of higher education to the poor and the disadvantaged. There is ample evidence from the developments cited that our time will be known as a period of great concern for improving learning techniques and for the application of technology in education.

CASE STUDIES

In addition to some of the developments cited as innovational in the study, there are many colleges that are attempting a redefinition and redevelopment of their total program. Of the 882 colleges that responded and were used in the sample in the study, 424 or 48.1 per cent indicated that they thought they were innovative institutions. Of course, not all of them are as innovative as they think, but the list includes many colleges that are exciting institutions. In addition, among those colleges indicating that they were not innovative, some stated that they have some innovative departments. Science departments were mentioned most often as being innovative in nature (95 times), with English (53), education (51), foreign languages (39), social science (36), psychology (33), history (32), mathematics (22), fine arts (22), and religion (19) following in that order.

With this over-all picture in mind, let us describe some institutions which are representative of new approaches in higher education.

Pfeiffer College, North Carolina.   Young men and women who entered Pfeiffer College in the fall of 1968 found an exciting, challenging, and rewarding academic and campus life experience awaiting them. The college that semester launched a plan called AIM (Academic-Incentive-Motivation). It is a plan based on hours of study and research on the part of the faculty and administration, with some help from students. The goal of AIM is one approach by an accredited, four-year, church-related college to meet current and future educational needs in this age.

Pfeiffer is a private, four-year, coeducational, liberal arts college affiliated with the Methodist Church, with an enrollment limit of 1,000 students. Facilities for 800 resident students are available in the dormitories, the students coming largely from the Southeastern, Middle Atlantic, and Northeastern states.

Pfeiffer's AIM program centers around an approach which emphasizes such features as:

1.   Encouraging students to set their own pace toward graduation. Some students may complete their studies for a bachelor of arts degree in as little as two and a half years (without summer school). The average student will graduate in four years, but those who need or desire to move at a slower pace may do so without embarrassment.

2.   Offering a new measuring system. The traditional "letter grading system" and credit hours have been abolished. AIM measures progress under a unit system which recognizes quantity as well as quality of work done.

3.   Encouraging independent creative thinking. The lecture system has been drastically reduced and AIM specifically calls for seminars, tutorials, independent reading, experimentation, and reporting as designed and directed by the faculty in keeping with each student's special interests and career goals. The only course in the entire curriculum which all students are expected to take is logic. Competency in such areas as composition, rhetoric, and grammar will be achieved through prior training or through noncredit courses. Foreign language competency, where this is called for by career and/or graduate school requirements, may be met by passing a reading examination or by formal instruction at Pfeiffer. Similarly, AIM dispenses with other so-called "general requirements" frequently prescribed for all students under other curriculum patterns. AIM guards against narrow specialization by insisting that each student, in addition to his primary subject area (major), selected from many open choices, elect an opposite or complementary area of work. This is to provide him a mode of thought or world view quite different from that in his chosen major.

There are other aspects of AIM. The college repudiates examinations which largely involve responses calling for memorization of facts, figures, places, and names through objective tests. The philosophy of AIM is that essay and oral examinations, open-book and library-centered quizzes, as well as special projects, better enable students to demonstrate creativity, originality, judgment, and organizational ability. AIM also provides the opportunity for students to earn extra units of credit where units earned during the regular term are below normal. Individual study and research during holiday and summer periods are involved. Finally, the individual student is counseled and guided in his academic program by a faculty member who is a specialist in the field the student wishes to enter.

Nasson College, Maine. New College, a division of Nasson College, opened in the fall of 1966 with a group of specially selected students who were offered a program and an atmosphere that was distinct from the traditional college academic program. The New College of Nasson College has no grades, a flexible curriculum, and lots of time for independent study. A student graduating from the New College receives a written summary of his accomplishments rather than the normal record of letter grades. The school's academic program is divided into seven provinces of knowledge, broad areas of the liberal arts that relate several disciplines. These include physical science, biological science, mathematics and logic, social science, behavioral science, arts and letters, and mind and spirit. These seven provinces of knowledge were evolved from the traditional disciplines in the following manner: Physical science from physics, chemistry, and earth science; biological science from biology, botany, and zoology; mathematics and logic from mathematics and logic; social science from history, government, geography, and economics; behavioral science from psychology, sociology, and cultural anthropology; arts and letters from art, esthetics, literature, and music; mind and spirit from philosophy and religions.

Each of the seven provinces contains essential related elements from several disciplines, selected and grouped because the study of those disciplines requires similar skills, knowledge, and modes of thought. For example, in the province of physical science it is not argued that physics and chemistry are the same; obviously they are not. Nor is it sufficient that chemistry and earth science overlap and interact in their subject matter—although indeed they do. Rather, the province of physical science is offered because there is an aggregate of skills, tools of scholarship, and modes of thinking which are germane to several disciplines—namely, physics, chemistry, and earth science. The interconnectedness of knowledge considered here is also apparent in the other provinces offered by the college.

The New College has four distinct and important reasons for organizing the curriculum along these provinces of knowledge. They are: (1) to reject the general education-specialization dualism; (2) to achieve greater integration through in-depth presentation of knowledge; (3) to develop more options for later specialization; and (4) to emphasize the kinds and aspects of knowledge which are most applicable to the acquisition of further knowledge and the development of wisdom. There are no required courses, as such, in order to eliminate the common division between general education and specialization. Students will pursue a province in progressively advanced form. A student may drop any of the provinces to which he is not suited, but to remain in school he must be able to progress in at least one province. What the province idea means is that one professor has to teach in one course what in other colleges is divided into several courses. Nevertheless, the college believes the student receives more in-depth instruction because various disciplines are constantly related to one another.

The program that leads to the bachelor of arts degree permits each student considerable latitude in charting his academic direction and his pace. Independence is fostered by individual study both on and away from the campus, with the program including a semester in a developing Latin American country during the sophomore year. Except for intensive preparation in Spanish before going to South America, the trip involves no academic work for students. The dean of the college feels that living and working in a different culture is education enough.

San Francisco State College, California. During the years 1966 to 1968, San Francisco State College conducted a study of the nature and purposes of general education in the late twentieth century. The study was coincident with a change in general education requirements for students graduating from California state colleges. The final report was presented to the Academic Senate of San Francisco State College in the fall semester, 1968.

In the first section of the report, the General Education Committee observed that in their practices most American colleges define liberal education as some degree of fusion of special and general studies. In examining the implications of this definition for San Francisco State College, the committee suggested that one basic element in a bachelor's degree program should be "the provision for the encouragement and free development of each student's special interests and unique abilities; that each student should be free to explore, to discover the depth and range of his own intellectual and creative power and the dimension of his ignorance; that each student should be free to discover through special study an appreciation for the structure of ideas, and the power and beauty of ideas."[1] The committee further suggested that a student's liberal education should also include what the committee referred to as "general studies"—"creation of an expanded context for each student's exploration of his special interests and unique abilities."[2] The value of the expanded context would reside in its capacity for protecting each student from intellectual, aesthetic, social, and moral provincialism.

---

[1] "Toward a New General Studies Program for San Francisco State College," prepared by the *Ad Hoc* General Education Committee for The President and the Academic Senate. San Francisco State College, June 1968, p. 3.1.

[2] *Ibid.*

In translating the broad intentions into more particular educational aims, the committee recommended that the proper emphasis to be given to the development of general studies curricula was the "whole person" approach. This means that the most desirable educational program is one that "places its emphasis upon the individual student and the quality of his experience and tries to arrange an educational environment in which it is possible for the individual to find his own way toward full development; that is, we strongly support the interpretation of 'relevance' that aims at allowing and encouraging each student to relate personally to subject matter, professors, other students—to the whole milieu of studying and being that we hopefully call a college community within a larger community that is finally the world—and that defines the 'usefulness' of learning in personal rather than simply marketplace terms."[3]

The committee discarded the concept of a set pattern of course requirements devised after administering a battery of tests to a sampling of students in favor of an "individual program" approach with its emphasis on intensive advising. The committee recommended an elective approach to the new General Studies Program with emphasis on interdisciplinary approaches, independent study, and the use of Senior Integrative Seminars. The committee stressed the need for regarding the freshman year as an exploratory, adventuresome, "even audacious" period. They felt that after twelve years of relatively regimented education, many freshmen arrive on campuses looking forward to serious intellectual and aesthetic experiences and considerable independence. Unfortunately, these freshmen are too often disillusioned before the end of their first term. The committee strongly recommended that "the excitement, ambition and desire for independence of freshmen should be respected."

Fairhaven College, Washington.   Established in the fall of 1968, Fairhaven College is a cluster college of Western Washington State College. The cluster college concept grew out of the pressures that accompany massive growth. As a college grows the multiplying echelons of administrative authority increasingly separate the individual student from those who make institutional policy. The lines between the academic departments harden and faculty attention is increasingly diverted toward responsibilities other than those of teaching undergraduates. A college is, or ought to be, a community of scholars in which professors, who are seasoned scholars, work closely with students, who are apprentice scholars. But, because a sense of community is possible only within a unit small enough to provide for communication among the individuals within the

[3] *Ibid.*, p. 3.3.

group, the process of education, particularly liberal education, can deteriorate as the institution grows. Often this decline is obscured to outsiders by the institution's growing prestige as a research institute or by the greater visibility that results from size. But the students know.

The cluster college idea—which is being developed on a number of campuses across the country—offers an opportunity to restore the advantages of a small college while at the same time making full use of the superior facilities (better laboratories, larger libraries, and well-staffed academic departments) of a much larger institution. Fairhaven College is the first step toward the development of a version of the cluster college plan, adapted to the special needs of Western Washington State College. It seems likely that Western some day will become a university. Already it has an expanding graduate program and a professional program of teacher education with a long history.

Fairhaven's purpose is to provide a quality liberal education and create an atmosphere conducive to experimentation with curricula, teaching procedures, staffing arrangements, independent study, and the new educational technology. Fairhaven, which opened in temporary quarters, will move to its own academic and housing facilities in 1969. Its total enrollment will be 600 students who will live in a cluster of small residence halls (fifty students in each) located adjacent to the main campus. Students will receive instruction from both the Fairhaven faculty and the departmental faculties of Western.

The Fairhaven curriculum includes, in addition to required and elective courses and seminars, a series of educational opportunities and responsibilities which are outside the context of the classrooms. Independent study and close faculty-student contact are integral parts of the program. Three major subdivisions comprise the curricular program of Fairhaven students: the Fairhaven Program, Required Fairhaven Courses, and Area of Concentration. Under the Fairhaven Program the student, during his undergraduate career, works closely with a faculty tutor who assists him in planning and carrying out his academic activities. Although the course-credit system provides a convenient vehicle for some academic tasks, many other experiences are of greater benefit when they are conducted in other ways. The residential aspect of Fairhaven makes it possible to build into the student's program a variety of activities such as study and discussion with visiting scholars and artists, individual study areas in which the student has some particular interest, extensive field trips, participation in short seminars during the year, and involvement in some research or creative endeavor. In addition, each Fairhaven student must demonstrate his ability to express himself effectively in writing and in speaking. This phase also includes participation in a variety of other activities, such as student publications, athletics, music, and drama.

Although faculty tutors are responsible for advisement and instruction in certain areas, students do much of their work with other faculty whose seminars or areas of scholarship are especially appropriate. Each year, tutors will prepare a written summary and evaluation of their students' work. When students complete their studies at Fairhaven, each tutor, with a committee of Fairhaven faculty who have worked closely with the student, will provide an over-all evaluation.

A number of required courses are included in the curriculum. These include the Great Periods sequence, a mathematics-science sequence, and a series of seminars. The required seminars include those in behaviorial science, aesthetics, philosophy and religion, and a senior seminar.

The Area of Concentration, in most instances, is comprised of a major and minor taken at Western. Occasionally a tutor and student may work out a new concentration which can be made up of both Western and Fairhaven activities.

The basic assumptions of Fairhaven College which underlie the curriculum are that skillful teachers and intellectually curious students can construct courses, seminars, field trips, and other educational experiences that hold more relevance and interest to both than do conventional courses, and that maximum flexibility must be allowed in the planning and execution of such activities.

Albion College, Michigan. The Unit System (a unit described as one-fourth of the student's time), with an average student load being four units a semester and thirty-two units required for graduation, along with an accompanying reevaluation and revision of the entire curriculum, was established at Albion College during the fall semester 1967–68 after two years' study. During the period of the curriculum revision, every course in the catalog was evaluated. Some courses were dropped, some were combined, some were extended, and some new courses were added. A special provision of the new curriculum allows each student to choose two courses in which he will be given final grades of Pass or Fail. These courses may neither be in his major field nor replace a core requirement.

Under the unit system plan, a student is required to complete thirty-two units of academic work, plus two years of physical education service courses for graduation. The revised plan requires for a degree thirteen units of study as follows: one unit of Freshman English; two units of foreign language; two units of natural science with laboratory work; one unit of fine arts; one unit in non-Western or intercultural thought; one unit in religion; one unit in philosophy; two units in literature; one unit from sociology, anthropology, or psychology; and one unit from economics, political science, or history. Half-unit courses were introduced to accommodate some specialization in exceptional cases.

The faculty at Albion feel that with the new unit system students now have greater opportunity to pursue subjects in depth. Each student takes fewer courses and therefore has a smaller number of individual class preparations and examinations than in the past. The aim is to reduce the fragmentation of the student's time and effort and to allow him time for self-education, "a very important aspect of the learning process." The Albion faculty also hope that there will be more time for interaction of student with student and student with faculty. With fewer preparations, each faculty member also has more time to devote to research and to the improvement of teaching.

Albion emphasizes the seminar approach, directed study, and offers an honors program. Albion's Summer Honors College, which was inaugurated in 1964, is designed to enrich the educational experience of selected students and to contribute to the professional development of the faculty participants. This is accomplished by the mutual involvement of a faculty member and a small number of students in an intensive full-time study of some particular problem suggested by the instructor. In 1961 Albion established an overseas summer study program. A five-week study period at the University of Neuchâtel, Switzerland, conducted in English by European professors, is preceded by a preliminary tour and lectures in other European centers. Under the total program students may earn one and one-half units of degree credit.

Other Colleges.   An experimental college was established at Fordham University in New York in the summer of 1967. The college is small, residential, housed close to campus, and forms part of "big" Fordham as well as being a unit on its own. It consists of a small group of faculty and, initially, thirty freshmen, men and women, who live and work together as a community. The program envisions an admission of thirty each year, with a three-year degree course, including summers, leading to a bachelor of arts degree. The idea is twofold: first, to rethink, faculty and students together, what it means to learn and to teach, and how to think, in this day and age, "what subjects are important and what aren't, how to bring lives and learning to bear on one another"; second, "speaking in an image, to found a city, a *polis,* largely self-governing, which will center round a shared purpose of active learning and be also a place of commitment and friendship where people's lives, not just their minds alone, belong, and possessing, in however small a way, a community-wide and world-wide dimension appropriate to our time."

In 1964 Beloit College in Wisconsin introduced its flexible year-round calendar and eliminated its traditional freshman, sophomore, and other class designations substituting underclass, middleclass and upperclass classifications. The main asset of the calendar has been to provide a scaffolding for the new curriculum. An incoming student spends the first three terms on campus—almost a full calendar year, ending about the middle of August and including two two-week vacations. This provides an introduction to college life "in psychological, social, and intellectual depth not achievable in two semesters." During this first three-term year, the one required course each term is the underclass common course, which has replaced the Freshman English Composition course. In taking other courses during the underclass year—normally three each term—the student may begin his major, complete preparation for his mathematics and language proficiency examinations if he has not already passed them, take courses in preparation for area examinations if he wants to, or simply take electives. There are no requirements.

Each student must pass an area examination in each of three areas—the humanities, the natural sciences, and social sciences—before he graduates. The examinations reflect an emphasis that Beloit places on combining breadth and depth and stresses the interdisciplinary approach.

Following the underclass year, a student's next two academic credit terms may fall during any two of the next five terms. In most cases these credit terms will be on the Beloit campus, but they may be off the campus in one of Beloit's foreign seminars conducted by its own faculty, in a foreign program, or in a cooperative program of the Associated Colleges of the Midwest. During the two credit terms of the middleclass period, a student will begin or continue work in his major, continue to prepare for and take area examinations, and take electives. There are no requirements during this period.

At some point during the middleclass period of five terms, a student must take one field term. If he wishes, he may also spend one or both of his vacation terms in the field.

For most students, the three-term, upperclass period will be a required three terms of academic study. The three terms will usually be spent on the Beloit campus. The student graduates at the end of April, after eleven terms enrolled at Beloit: three underclass terms on campus, two middleclass credit terms, two vacation terms, a field term, and three upperclass credit terms that begin with the spring-summer term, go through the fall term, and close with commencement at the end of the winter term in April. In addition to completing work in his major field, completing whatever area examinations remain, and taking electives, a student has two requirements during the upperclass year: a one-term, upperclass common course to be taken either in the spring-summer term or the fall term, and a comprehensive examination in his major field.

"Under the Beloit Plan," says the college's president, Miller Upton, "a student is less concerned with accumulation of course credits and more concerned with true intellectual growth."

The small-college organization within a larger institution finds another clear expression in the Raymond and Covell Colleges of the University of the Pacific in California. At the University of California, Davis Campus, there is great interest in the development of the Experimental College, a program offering "experimental classes" outside the formal course structure of the university. The program was introduced in 1967. In 1966, a less radical departure was introduced called "Faculty 48's," courses offering credit toward graduation, with enrollment usually limited, and no necessary correlation between the course topic and the instructor's official departmental or discipline affiliation. Instructors volunteer out of enthusiasm for the idea, so that offerings for any given quarter fluctuate and are somewhat unpredictable.

Great changes in higher education are in progress. From every quarter evidence is suggesting that the 1970's will see vastly different colleges and universities than those of the 1960's. With the great influx of students, with the entry of both the government and large industrial concerns into the field, and with the many new media available, changes are taking place at a very rapid rate. We, as educators, cannot keep these changes from occurring, nor should we want to, but we can determine what these changes will be. If we do not move quickly the new directions may well be determined by those outside higher education, but if we will make our own new plans and patterns for developing more effective and more efficient instruction, then we can determine the changes ourselves.

SELECTED BIBLIOGRAPHY

ANDERSON, G. ERNEST, JR. "Estimated Time for Accepting Educational Ideas: 30 Years." *Nation's Schools*, 78:50, December 1966.

BARNETT, HOMER GARNER. *Innovation: The Basis of Cultural Change*. New York: McGraw-Hill Book Company, Inc., 1953. 462 pp.

BASKIN, SAMUEL, EDITOR. *Higher Education: Some Newer Developmens.* New York: McGraw-Hill Book Company, Inc., 1965. 342 pp.

BENNIS, WARREN G., KENNETH DEAN BENNE, AND ROBERT CHIN. *The Planning of Change: Readings in the Applied Behavioral Sciences*. New York: Holt, Rinehart and Winston, 1961. 781 pp.

BLOCK, A. H. "Philosophical Approaches and the New Media," *Improving College and University Teaching*, 14:32–35, Winter 1966.

BONTHIUS, ROBERT H., JAMES F. DAVIS, AND J. GARBER DRUSHAL. *The Independent Study Program in the United States*. New York: Columbia University Press, 1957. 259 pp.

BROWN, JAMES W., AND JAMES W. THORNTON, JR. *New Media in Higher Education*. Washington, D.C.: Association for Higher Education, 1963. 182 pp.

CARLSON, RICHARD O. *Adoption of Educational Innovations*. Oregon: University of Oregon Press, 1965. 84 pp.

CHEN, WEN CHAO. "A Sound Library Service for the Small College." *Liberal Education*, 46:233–240, May 1960.

DIETRICH, JOHN E., TED W. WARD, AND HORACE C. HARTSELL. "Media Development: A Part of Instructional Change." *Audiovisual Instruction*, 10:393–395, May 1965.

143

DYKES, ARCHIE R. "Innovation in Higher Education." *School and Society,* 94:179–181, April 2, 1966.

Educational Television: The Next Ten Years. Stanford: Institute for Communication Research, 1962. 375 pp.

EURICH, ALVIN C. "The Commitment to Experiment and Innovate in College Teaching." *Educational Record,* 45:49–50, Winter 1964.

HEYWOOD, STANLEY J. "Toward A Sound Theory of Innovation." *Elementary School Journal,* 66:107–114, December 1965.

Innovation and Experiment in Education. A Progress Report of the Panel on Educational Research and Development to the U.S. Commissioner of Education, the Director of the National Science Foundation, and the Special Assistant to the President for Science and Technology. Washington, D.C.: Government Printing Office, 1964. 74 pp.

JOHNSON, B. LAMAR. *Islands of Innovation,* UCLA Junior College Leadership Program, Occasional Report No. 6. Los Angeles: University of California, School of Education, 1964. 80 pp.

LEYDEN, RALPH C. *10 Years of Closed Circuit TV at Stephens College, 1955–1965.* Missouri: Stephens College, 1966. 115 pp.

MAYHEW, LEWIS B. *The Collegiate Curriculum: An Approach to Analysis.* Research Monograph No. 11. Atlanta, Ga.: Southern Regional Education Board, 1966. 38 pp.

McIRVINE, EDWARD, *et al. Dialogue on Technology.* Indianapolis, Ind.: Bobbs-Merrill Co., Inc., 1967. 109 pp.

MERZ, WILLIAM R. "Education and the Process of Change." *Educational Leadership,* 24:561–567, March 1967.

MILES, MATTHEW B., EDITOR. *Innovation in Education.* New York: Teachers College Press, Teachers College, Columbia University, 1964. 689 pp.

MILLER, PAUL A. "Clearing the Way for Innovation." *Educational Record,* 48:138–143, Spring 1967.

Non-Western Studies in the Liberal Arts College. A Report of the Commission on International Understanding. Washington, D.C.: Association of American Colleges, 1964. 362 pp.

PARKER, W. W. "Library in the Liberal Arts College." *College and Research Libraries,* 16:177–182, April 1955.

ROGERS, EVERETT M. *Diffusion of Innovations.* New York: The Free Press, 1962. 367 pp.

SCHRAMM, WILBUR. *The Research on Programmed Instruction, An Annotated Bibliography.* Washington, D.C.: Government Printing Office, 1964. 114 pp.

SHORES, LOUIS, ROBERT JORDAN, AND JOHN HARVEY. *The Library-College.* Philadelphia: Drexel Press, 1966. 278 pp.

TAUBER, MAURICE F., AND IRLENE R. STEPHENS, EDITORS. *Conference on the Use of Printed and Audio-Visual Materials for Instructional Purposes.* New York: Columbia University, 1966.

THEOBALD, ROBERT. "Higher Education and Cybernation; with reply by R. W. Tyler." *NEA Journal,* 55:26–29, March 1966.

TRAXLER, ARTHUR E. *Innovation and Experiment in Modern Education.* Washington, D.C.: American Council on Education, 1965. 159 pp.

UNITED STATES DEPARTMENT OF HEALTH, EDUCATION, AND WELFARE. *Approach to Independent Study.* Compiled by Winslow R. Hatch and Alice L. Richards. Washington, D.C.: Government Printing Office, 1964. 114 pp.

WERDELL, PHILIP. *Course and Teacher Evaluation.* Washington, D.C.: United States National Student Association, 1967. 104 pp.

Appendix A

SURVEY OF INNOVATIVE PRACTICES

in

Colleges of Arts and Sciences

Please fill out the enclosed questionnaire as completely as possible. Wherever you think you may wish to expand on your statements, please feel free to attach additional comments. We would appreciate receiving any descriptive material to supplement your responses. As soon as you have completed the questionnaire, please return it to:

> Institute of Higher Education
> Teachers College, Columbia University
> 525 West 120th Street
> New York, New York 10027

Thank you very much for your cooperation.

A. IDENTIFYING INFORMATION

Name of college ....

Address ....

Student enrollment (Full-time undergraduate) ....

No. of faculty (Full-time equivalent) ....

Form completed by .... Title ....

Name or names of persons on staff to whom further inquiries concerning particular practices might be sent, if other than person completing form

....

....

147

DIRECTIONS

Below is a list of educational practices.

In Column A indicate by check (√) whether in your estimation you are doing anything innovative or unusual in this area, or if you are planning to do anything innovative or unusual in the near future. For the purpose of this study *innovation is defined* as a new practice or procedure for your institution.

In Column B indicate by check (√) the time of the introduction of the innovative practice.

In Column C indicate by check (√) how widespread the innovative practice is. Is it college wide, in certain departments only, or is the practice engaged in by a few innovative individuals?

| | COLUMN A | | COLUMN B | | | COLUMN C | | |
| | | | Introduced Introduced Planning | | | | | |
	Yes	No	prior to 1961	in 1961 or After	to Introduce	College-wide	Dept.	Indiv-idual
B. CURRICULUM AND INSTRUCTION								
Use of Teaching Aides	: :	: :	: :	: :	: :	: :	: :	: :
Team Teaching	: :	: :	: :	: :	: :	: :	: :	: :
Independent Study:								
For Superior Students Only	: :	: :	: :	: :	: :	: :	: :	: :
For All Students	: :	: :	: :	: :	: :	: :	: :	: :
Use of Educational TV	: :	: :	: :	: :	: :	: :	: :	: :
Use of Programmed Instruction	: :	: :	: :	: :	: :	: :	: :	: :
Use of Teaching Machines	: :	: :	: :	: :	: :	: :	: :	: :
Work-Study Program	: :	: :	: :	: :	: :	: :	: :	: :
Projects Involving Local Community	: :	: :	: :	: :	: :	: :	: :	: :
Undergraduate Study Abroad	: :	: :	: :	: :	: :	: :	: :	: :
Off-campus Study in U.S.	: :	: :	: :	: :	: :	: :	: :	: :
Use of Dormitory as a Learning Center	: :	: :	: :	: :	: :	: :	: :	: :
Freshman Seminars	: :	: :	: :	: :	: :	: :	: :	: :
Honors Programs	: :	: :	: :	: :	: :	: :	: :	: :

Interdisciplinary Studies ....

Language Laboratories ....

Interinstitutional Cooperative Programs ....

Non-Western Studies ....

Programs for Special Students:

Programs for Slow Learners ....

Remedial Programs ....

Programs for Exceptional Students ....

Programs for Dropouts ....

Special Programs for Women ....

Special Extension Programs ....

Special Adult Education Programs ....

Variations in Faculty Characteristics:

Artists in Residence ....

Other Specialists in Residence ....

Other Practices or Procedures

(Please List) ....

C. STUDENT SERVICES AND STUDENT
EVALUATION

Advanced Placement Program ....

Special Examinations for Admissions ....

Early Identification of Gifted ....

Articulation with High Schools ....

Other Variations in Admissions ....

Student Participation on Faculty Committees ....

Student Involvement in Governance ....

Student Involvement in Faculty Selection ....

Student Involvement in Faculty Evaluation ....

Variations in Guidance Services ....

Variations in Health Services ....

149

| | COLUMN A | | COLUMN B | | | COLUMN C | | |
	Yes	No	Introduced prior to 1961	Introduced in 1961 or After	Planning to Introduce	College-wide	Dept.	Individual
Student Housing Programs								
Living-Learning Residence Halls	......	......	......	......	......	......	......	......
Cocurricular Activities	......	......	......	......	......	......	......	......
Comprehensive Examinations	......	......	......	......	......	......	......	......
Variations in Grading Practices	......	......	......	......	......	......	......	......
Other Practices or Procedures								
(Please List)	......	......	......	......	......	......	......	......
D. ORGANIZATION AND STRUCTURE								
Substitutes for Traditional Calendar:								
Quarter	......	......	......	......	......	......	......	......
Trimester	......	......	......	......	......	......	......	......
Other	......	......	......	......	......	......	......	......
New Campus Plans	......	......	......	......	......	......	......	......
New Styles in Classrooms	......	......	......	......	......	......	......	......
Experimentation in Cost-planning	......	......	......	......	......	......	......	......
New Styles in Governance	......	......	......	......	......	......	......	......
New Styles in Libraries:								
Use of Librarians	......	......	......	......	......	......	......	......
Library Facilities	......	......	......	......	......	......	......	......
Use of Automation in Library	......	......	......	......	......	......	......	......
Library as Learning Resource Center	......	......	......	......	......	......	......	......
Library-Teacher Relationships	......	......	......	......	......	......	......	......
E. OTHER EDUCATIONAL PRACTICES								
PLEASE LIST	......	......	......	......	......	......	......	......

F. GENERAL QUESTIONS

1. Would you characterize your college
   as innovative?   Yes...... No......

2. If answer is no, would you characterize
   any of your departments as innovative?   Yes...... No......
   If yes, which ones? Why?

3. Please identify innovative faculty on your campus.

4. If you are a church-related institution, have you made or are you
   contemplating any innovative relationships with parent church
   body?   Yes......No......
   If yes, please describe.

Of the practices introduced since 1961 on your campus, could you list and describe the practices at your institution which you consider most imaginative, novel or vital? A short descriptive paragraph of these practices would suffiice.

Please send us any documents, statements or materials which would describe or explain any of the innovative or experimental practices on your campus.

Thank you very much for your time and effort.

Appendix B

COOPERATING COLLEGES

ALABAMA
 Alabama Agricultural and Mechanical College, Normal
 Alabama College, Montevallo
 Alabama State College, Montgomery
 Athens College, Athens
 Birmingham-Southern College, Birmingham
 Florence State College, Florence
 Huntingdon College, Montgomery
 Judson College, Marion
 Livingston State College, Livingston
 Miles College, Birmingham
 Oakwood College, Huntsville
 Saint Bernard College, St. Bernard
 Samford University, Birmingham
 Spring Hill College, Mobile
 Talladega College, Talladega
 Troy State College, Troy
 Tuskegee Institute, Tuskegee Institute
 University of Alabama, University
 University of South Alabama, Mobile

ALASKA
 Alaska Methodist University, Anchorage
 University of Alaska, College

ARIZONA
 Arizona State University, Tempe
 Grand Canyon College, Phoenix
 Northern Arizona University, Flagstaff
 University of Arizona, Tucson

ARKANSAS

Arkansas Agricultural, Mechanical, and Normal College, Pine Bluff
Arkansas Agricultural and Mechanical College, College Heights
Arkansas College, Batesville
Arkansas Polytechnic College, Russellville
Arkansas State University, State College
Arkansas State Teachers College, Conway
Harding College, Searcy
Henderson State Teachers College, Arkadelphia
Hendrix College, Conway
John Brown University, Siloam Springs
Little Rock University, Little Rock
Philander Smith College, Little Rock
Southern State College, Magnolia
The College of the Ozarks, Clarksville
University of Arkansas, Fayetteville

CALIFORNIA

Azusa Pacific College, Azusa
California Baptist College, Riverside
California Institute of Arts, Los Angeles
California Lutheran College, Thousand Oaks
California State College at Fullerton
California State College at Hayward
California State College at Long Beach
California State Polytechnic College, San Luis Obispo
Chapman College, Orange
Chico State College, Chico
Claremont Men's College, Claremont
College of Notre Dame, Belmont
Fresno State College, Fresno
Golden Gate College, San Francisco
Humboldt State College, Arcata
Immaculate Heart College, Los Angeles
Loyola University, Los Angeles
Marymount College, Palos Verdes Estates
Mills College, Oakland
Monterey Institute of Foreign Studies, Monterey
Mount St. Mary's College, Los Angeles
Occidental College, Los Angeles
Pacific Union College, Angwin
Pasadena College, Pasadena
Pepperdine College, Los Angeles
Pitzer College, Claremont
Pomona College, Claremont
St. John's College, Camarillo
St. Joseph's College of Orange, Orange
San Diego State College, San Diego
San Fernando Valley State College, Northridge

San Francisco College for Women, San Francisco
San Francisco State College, San Francisco
San Jose State College, San Jose
San Luis Rey College, San Luis Rey
Scripps College, Claremont
Sonoma State College, Rhonert Park
Stanford University, Stanford
Stanislaus State College, Turlock
University of California, Berkeley
University of California, Davis
University of California, San Diego
University of California, Santa Barbara
University of the Pacific, Stockton
  Raymond College
  Elbert Covell College
University of Redlands, Redlands
University of San Diego, College for Men, San Diego
University of Santa Clara, Santa Clara
University of Southern California, Los Angeles
Westmont College, Santa Barbara

COLORADO

Adams State College, Alamosa
Colorado College, Colorado Springs
Colorado State University, Fort Collins
Colorado Woman's College, Denver
Fort Lewis College, Durango
Loretto Heights College, Denver
Regis College, Denver
Southern Colorado State College, Pueblo
United States Air Force Academy, Colorado Springs
University of Colorado, Boulder

CONNECTICUT

Albertus Magnus College, New Haven
Annhurst College, Woodstock
Central Connecticut State College, New Britain
Connecticut College, New London
Danbury State College, Danbury
Fairfield University, Fairfield
Sacred Heart University, Bridgeport
Saint Alphonsus College, Suffield
Saint Joseph College, West Hartford
Southern Connecticut State College, New Haven
Trinity College, Hartford
University of Bridgeport, Bridgeport
University of Hartford, West Hartford
Wesleyan University, Middletown
Yale University, New Haven

DELAWARE

>Delaware State College, Dover
>University of Delaware, Newark

DISTRICT OF COLUMBIA

>The American University
>Catholic University of America
>Dunbarton College of Holy Cross
>George Washington University
>St. Paul's College
>Trinity College

FLORIDA

>Barry College, Miami
>Bethune-Cookman College, Daytona Beach
>Florida Agricultural and Mechanical University, Tallahassee
>Florida Atlantic University, Boca Raton
>Florida Memorial College, Saint Augustine
>Florida Presbyterian College, Saint Petersburg
>Florida Southern College, Lakeland
>Florida State University, Tallahassee
>Jacksonville University, Jacksonville
>Rollins College, Winter Park
>South-Eastern Bible College, Inc., Lakeland
>University of Florida, Gainesville
>University of South Florida, Tampa
>University of Tampa, Tampa

GEORGIA

>Albany State College, Albany
>Berry College, Mount Berry
>Brenau College, Gainesville
>Clark College, Atlanta
>Emory College, Emory University, Atlanta
>Georgia Southern College, Statesboro
>Georgia State College, Atlanta
>LaGrange College, LaGrange
>Morehouse College, Atlanta
>North Georgia College, Dahlonega
>Oglethorpe College, Atlanta
>Paine College, Augusta
>Shorter College, Rome
>Tift College, Forsyth
>Franklin College of Arts & Sciences, University of Georgia, Athens
>Valdosta State College, Valdosta
>Wesleyan College, Macon
>West Georgia College, Carrollton
>The Woman's College of Georgia, Milledgeville

GUAM
>College of Guam, Agana

HAWAII
>University of Hawaii, College of Arts & Sciences, Honolulu

IDAHO
>The College of Idaho, Caldwell
>Northwest Nazarene College, Nampa
>University of Idaho, Moscow

ILLINOIS
>Augustana College, Rock Island
>Aurora College, Aurora
>Barat College, Lake Forest
>Blackburn College, Carlinville
>Bradley University, Peoria
>The College of Jewish Studies, Chicago
>College of St. Francis, Joliet
>Eastern Illinois University, Charleston
>Elmhurst College, Elmhurst
>Eureka College, Eureka
>Greenville College, Greenville
>Illinois College, Jacksonville
>Illinois Wesleyan University, Bloomington
>Judson College, Elgin
>Knox College, Galesburg
>Lake Forest College, Lake Forest
>Lewis College, Lockport
>Loyola University, Chicago
>McKendree College, Lebanon
>MacMurray College, Jacksonville
>Maryknoll College, Glen Ellyn
>Millikin University, Decatur
>Monmouth College, Monmouth
>Mundelein College, Chicago
>North Central College, Naperville
>North Park College, Chicago
>Northwestern University, College of Arts & Sciences, Evanston
>Olivet Nazarene College, Kankakee
>Principia College, Elsah
>Quincy College, Quincy
>Rockford College, Rockford
>Rosary College, River Forest
>St. Procopius College, Lisle
>St. Xavier College, Chicago
>Southern Illinois University, Carbondale
>Southern Illinois University, Edwardsville
>Trinity College, Deerfield

University of Chicago, The College, Chicago
University of Illinois, Chicago
University of Illinois, Urbana
Wheaton College, Wheaton

INDIANA

Anderson College, Anderson
Ball State University, Muncie
Bethel College, Mishawaka
Concordia Senior College, Fort Wayne
DePauw University, Greencastle
Earlham College, Richmond
Fort Wayne Bible College, Fort Wayne
Goshen College, Goshen
Grace College, Winona Lake
Hanover College, Hanover
Huntington College, Huntington
Indiana Central College, Indianapolis
Indiana State University, Terre Haute
Marion College, Marion
Oakland City College, Oakland City
Saint Francis College, Fort Wayne
Saint Joseph's College, Rensselaer
Saint Mary-of-the-Woods College, Saint Mary-of-the-Woods
St. Meinrad College, St. Meinrad
Taylor University, Upland
University of Evansville, Evansville
University of Norte Dame, Notre Dame
Wabash College, Crawfordsville

IOWA

Briar Cliff College, Sioux City
Buena Vista College, Storm Lake
Central College, Pella
Clarke College, Dubuque
Cornell College, Mount Vernon
Dordt College, Sioux Center
Drake University, Des Moines
Graceland College, Lamoni
Grinnell College, Grinnell
Iowa State University of Science & Technology, Ames
Iowa Wesleyan College, Mount Pleasant
Loras College, Dubuque
Luther College, Decorah
Morningside College, Sioux City
Mount Mercy College, Cedar Rapids
Northwestern College, Orange City
Parsons College, Fairfield
Simpson College, Indianola

State College of Iowa, Cedar Falls
The University of Iowa, Iowa City
Upper Iowa College, Fayette
Wartburg College, Waverly
Westmar College, LeMars
William Penn College, Oskaloosa

KANSAS

Baker University, Baldwin City
Bethany College, Lindsborg
The College of Emporia, Emporia
Fort Hays Kansas State College, Hays
Friends University, Wichita
Kansas State College of Pittsburg, Pittsburg
Kansas State Teachers College, Emporia
Kansas Wesleyan University, Salina
Marymount College, Salina
McPherson College, McPherson
Ottawa University, Ottawa
St. Benedict's College, Atchison
Saint Mary College, Xavier
Saint Mary of the Plains College, Dodge City
Southwestern College, Winfield
Sterling College, Sterling
Tabor College, Hillsboro
The University of Kansas, Lawrence
Washburn University of Topeka, Topeka

KENTUCKY

Bellarmine College, Louisville
Brescia College, Owensboro
Campbellsville College, Campbellsville
Catherine Spalding College, Louisville
Centre College of Kentucky, Danville
Eastern Kentucky University, Richmond
Georgetown College, Georgetown
Kentucky State College, Frankfort
Kentucky Wesleyan College, Owensboro
Morehead State University, Morehead
Murray State University, Murray
Nazareth College of Kentucky, Nazareth
Transylvania College, Lexington
Union College, Barbourville
Ursuline College, Louisville
Villa Madonna, Covington
Western Kentucky University, Bowling Green

LOUISIANA

Centenary College of Louisiana, Shreveport
Dillard University, New Orleans

Grambling College, Grambling
Louisiana College, Pineville
Louisiana Polytechnic Institute, Ruston
Louisiana State University, Baton Rouge
Loyola University, New Orleans
McNeese State College, Lake Charles
Northeast Louisiana State College, Monroe
Northwestern State College of Louisiana, Natchitoches
Xavier University of New Orleans, New Orleans

MAINE

Bates College, Lewiston
Bowdoin College, Brunswick
Colby College, Waterville
Nasson College, Springvale
Ricker College, Houston
Saint Francis College, Biddeford
Saint Joseph's College, North Windham
University of Maine, Orono

MARYLAND

Bowie State College, Bowie
College of Notre Dame of Maryland, Inc., Baltimore
Columbia Union College, Takoma Park
Frostburg State College, Frostburg
Goucher College, Baltimore
Hood College, Frederick
Loyola College, Baltimore
Morgan State College, Baltimore
Mount Saint Agnes College, Baltimore
Mount Saint Mary's College, Emmitsburg
Saint John's College, Annapolis
    Santa Fe, New Mexico Campus
Saint Joseph College, Emmitsburg
Saint Mary's Seminary College, Baltimore
Salisbury State College, Salisbury
University of Baltimore, Baltimore
Washington College, Chestertown
Western Maryland College, Westminster

MASSACHUSETTS

American International College, Springfield
Amherst College, Amherst
Anna Maria College for Women, Paxton
Assumption College, Worcester
Atlantic Union College, South Lancaster
Boston College, Newton
Boston University, College of Liberal Arts, Boston
Brandeis University, Waldham
Cardinal Cushing College, Brookline

Clark University, Worcester
College of the Holy Cross, Worcester
Curry College, Milton
Eastern Nazarene College, Wallaston
Emerson College, Boston
Gordon College, Wenham
Harvard College, Cambridge
Merrimack College, North Andover
Mount Alvernia College, Newton
Northeastern University, Boston
Regis College for Women, Weston
Simmons College, Boston
Smith College, Northampton
Southeastern Massachusetts Technological Institute, North Dartmouth
Springfield College, Springfield
State College at Boston, Boston
State College, Salem
Stonehill College, North Easton
Suffolk University, Boston
Tufts University, Medford
Wellesley College, Wellesley
Williams College, Williamstown

MICHIGAN

Adrian College, Adrian
Albion College, Albion
Alma College, Alma
Andrews University, Berrien Springs
Aquinas College, Grand Rapids
Calvin College, Grand Rapids
Central Michigan University, Mt. Pleasant
The Detroit Institute of Technology, Detroit
Duns Scotus College, Southfield
Grand Valley State College, Allendale
Hillsdale College, Hillsdale
Hope College, Holland
Kalamazoo College, Kalamazoo
Madonna College, Livonia
Marygrove College, Detroit
Mercy College of Detroit, Detroit
Michigan State University, East Lansing
Nazareth College, Nazareth
Owosso College, Owosso
Sacred Heart Seminary, Detroit
Siena Heights College, Adrian
University of Detroit, Detroit
University of Michigan, Ann Arbor
Wayne State University, Detroit
Western Michigan University, Kalamazoo

MINNESOTA

Augsburg College, Minneapolis
Bemidji State College, Bemidji
Bethel College, St. Paul
Carleton College, Northfield
College of Saint Benedict, Saint Joseph
The College of Saint Catherine, St. Paul
College of Saint Scholastica, Duluth
College of Saint Teresa, Winona
Concordia College, St. Paul
Gustavus Adolphus College, St. Peter
Hamline University, St. Paul
Macalester College, St. Paul
Mankato State College, Mankato
Northwestern College, Minneapolis
Saint Cloud State College, Saint Cloud
Saint John's University, Collegeville
Saint Mary's College, Winona
Saint Olaf College, Northfield
University of Minnesota, Minneapolis

MISSISSIPPI

Delta State College, Cleveland
Jackson State College, Jackson
Mississippi College, Clinton
Mississippi State College for Women, Columbus
Mississippi State University, State College
Mississippi Valley State College, Itta Bena
Rust College, Holly Springs
The University of Mississippi, University
University of Southern Mississippi, Hattiesburg
William Carey College, Hattiesburg

MISSOURI

Avila College, Kansas City
Cardinal Glennon College, St. Louis
Central Missouri State College, Warrensburg
Culver-Stockton College, Canton
Drury College, Springfield
Evangel College, Springfield
Fontbonne College, St. Louis
Lindenwood College, St. Charles
Marillac College, St. Louis
Missouri Valley College, Marshall
Northeast Missouri State College, Kirksville
Northwest Missouri State College, Maryville
Notre Dame College, St. Louis
Rockhurst College, Kansas City

Saint Mary's Seminary, Perryville
Southeast Missouri State College, Cape Girardeau
Southwest Missouri State College, Springfield
Stephens College, Columbia
Tarkio College, Tarkio
University of Missouri, Columbia Campus
   Kansas City Campus
   St. Louis Campus
Washington University, St. Louis
Webster College, St. Louis
Westminster College, Fulton
William Jewell College, Liberty

MONTANA

   Carroll College, Helena
   Eastern Montana College, Billings
   Montana State University, Bozeman
   Rocky Mountain College, Billings

NEBRASKA

   Chadron State College, Chadron
   The College of Saint Mary, Omaha
   Creighton University, Omaha
   Dana College, Blair
   Duchesne College, Omaha
   Hastings College, Hastings
   Kearney State College, Kearney
   Midland Lutheran College, Fremont
   Municipal University of Omaha, Omaha
   Nebraska Wesleyan University, Lincoln
   Union College, Lincoln
   University of Nebraska, Lincoln

NEW HAMPSHIRE

   Franklin Pierce College, Rindge
   Mount Saint Mary College, Hooksett
   New England College, Henniker
   Plymouth State College of the University of New Hampshire, Plymouth
   Rivier College, Nashua
   Saint Anselm's College, Manchester
   University of New Hampshire, Durham

NEW JERSEY

   Alma White College, Zarephath
   Bloomfield College, Bloomfield
   Caldwell College for Women, Caldwell
   College of Saint Elizabeth, Convent Station
   Don Bosco College, Newton

Drew University, Madison
Fairleigh Dickinson University, Rutherford
Princeton University, Princeton
Rider College, Trenton
Rutgers University, New Brunswick
Saint Peter's College, Jersey City
Seton Hall University, South Orange
Upsala College, East Orange

NEW MEXICO

College of Santa Fe, Santa Fe
College of the Southwest, Hobbs
Eastern New Mexico University, Portales
New Mexico Highlands University, Las Vegas
New Mexico State University, University Park
University of Albuquerque, Albuquerque

NEW YORK

Bard College, Annandale-on-Hudson
Barnard College, Columbia University, New York City
Brooklyn College, City University of New York, Brooklyn
Canisius College, Buffalo
City College, City University of New York, New York City
Colgate University, Hamilton
College of Mount Saint Vincent, Bronx, New York City
College of Saint Rose, Albany
Columbia College, Columbia University, New York City
Cornell University, Ithaca
D'Youville College, Buffalo
Elmira College, Elmira
Finch College, New York City
Fordham University, Bronx, New York City
Hamilton College, Clinton
Hartwick College, Oneonta
Hobart and William Smith Colleges, Geneva
Hofstra University, Hempstead
Hunter College, City University of New York, New York City
Iona College, New Rochelle
Ithaca College, Ithaca
Keuka College, Keuka Park
King's College, Briarcliff Manor
Ladycliff College, Highland Falls
Le Moyne College, Syracuse
Long Island University
    C. W. Post Campus, Brookville
    Southampton Campus, Greenvale
Manhattan College, Bronx, New York City
Manhattanville College of the Sacred Heart, Purchase
Marist College, Poughkeepsie

Mary Rogers College, Maryknoll
Marymount Manhattan College, New York City
Mercy College, Dobbs Ferry
Molloy Catholic College for Women, Rockville Centre
Mount Saint Mary College, Newburgh
New York University, Bronx, New York City
Niagara University, Niagara University
Pace College, New York City
Roberts Wesleyan College, North Chili
Rosary Hill College, Buffalo
Russell Sage College, Troy
Saint Bonaventure University, St. Bonaventure
Saint Francis College, Brooklyn
Saint John Fisher College, Rochester
Saint John's University, Jamaica
Saint Lawrence University, Canton
Siena College, Loudonville
State University of New York
   College at Buffalo
   College at Cortland
   College at Fredonia
   College at Geneseo
   College at Oswego
   College at Potsdam
   University at Albany
   University at Binghamton
   University at Buffalo
   University at Stony Brook
Syracuse University, Syracuse
Union College and University, Schenectady
Utica College, Utica
Vassar College, Poughkeepsie
Wagner College, Staten Island
Wells College, Aurora
Yeshiva University, New York City
Yeshiva University, Stern College for Women, New York City

NORTH CAROLINA

Appalachian State Teachers College, Boone
Atlantic Christian College, Wilson
Belmont Abbey College, Belmont
Bennett College, Greensboro
Catawba College, Salisbury
Davidson College, Davidson
East Carolina College, Greenville
Elon College, Elon
Greensboro College, Greensboro
Guilford College, Greensboro
High Point College, High Point

Johnson C. Smith University, Charlotte
Lenoir Rhyne College, Hickory
Livingstone College, Salisbury
Meredith College, Raleigh
Methodist College, Fayetteville
North Carolina College at Durham, Durham
North Carolina Wesleyan College, Rocky Mount
Pembroke State College, Pembroke
Pfeiffer College, Misenheimer
Queens College, Charlotte
Saint Andrews Presbyterian College, Laurinburg
Saint Augustine's College, Raleigh
Salem College, Winston-Salem
Shaw University, Raleigh
University of North Carolina at Greensboro, Greensboro
Western Carolina College, Cullowhee
Wilmington College, Wilmington
Winston-Salem State College, Winston-Salem

NORTH DAKOTA

Jamestown College, Jamestown
Mary College, Bismarck
Mayville State College, Mayville
Minot State College, Minot
University of North Dakota, Grand Forks
Valley City State College, Valley City

OHIO

Antioch College, Yellow Springs
Athenaeum of Ohio, Norwood
Baldwin-Wallace College, Berea
Bluffton College, Bluffton
Bowling Green State University, Bowling Green
Capital University, Columbus
Cleveland State University, Cleveland
College of St. Mary of the Springs, Columbus
College of Steubenville, Steubenville
College of Wooster, Wooster
Defiance College, Defiance
Denison University, Granville
Findlay College, Findlay
Heidelberg College, Tiffin
Hiram College, Hiram
Kent State University, Kent
Kenyon College, Gambier
Lake Erie College, Painesville
Malone College, Canton
Marietta College, Marietta
Mary Manse College, Toledo

Mount Union College, Alliance
Muskingum College, New Concord
Oberlin College, Oberlin
Ohio Northern University, Ada
Ohio University, Athens
Ohio Wesleyan University, Delaware
Otterbein College, Westerville
Our Lady of Cincinnati College, Cincinnati
Pontifical College Josephinum, Worthington
Rio Grande College, Rio Grande
University of Akron, Akron
University of Cincinnati, Cincinnati
University of Dayton, Dayton
Ursuline College for Women, Cleveland
Western College for Women, Oxford
Western Reserve University, Cleveland
Wilmington College, Wilmington
Wittenberg University, Springfield
Xavier University, Cincinnati

OKLAHOMA

Central State College, Edmond
Langston University, Langston
Northeastern State College, Tahlequah
Northwestern State College, Alva
Oklahoma Baptist University, Shawnee
Oklahoma Christian College, Oklahoma City
Oklahoma City University, Oklahoma City
Oklahoma College of Liberal Arts, Chickasha
Oklahoma State University, Stillwater
Panhandle Agricultural and Mechanical College, Goodwell
Phillips University, Enid
Southeastern State College, Durant
University of Tulsa, Tulsa

OREGON

Eastern Oregon College, La Grande
George Fox College, Newberg
Linfield College, McMinnville
Mount Angel College, Mount Angel
Northwest Christian College, Eugene
Oregon State University, Corvallis
Pacific University, Forest Grove
Portland State College, Portland
Reed College, Portland
Southern Oregon College, Ashland
University of Portland, Portland
Warner Pacific College, Portland
Willamette University, Salem

PENNSYLVANIA

Albright College, Reading
Allegheny College, Meadville
Alliance College, Cambridge Springs
Beaver College, Glenside
Bloomsburg State College, Bloomsburg
Bryn Mawr College, Bryn Mawr
Bucknell University, Lewisburg
Cabrini College, Radnor
California State College, California
Chatham College, Pittsburgh
Clarion State College, Clarion
College Misericordia, Dallas
Dickinson College, Carlisle
East Stroudsburg State College, East Stroudsburg
Eastern Baptist College, St. Davids
Eastern Pilgrim College, Allentown
Edinboro State College, Edinboro
Elizabethtown College, Elizabethtown
Franklin and Marshall College, Lancaster
Gannon College, Erie
Geneva College, Beaver Falls
Gettysburg College, Gettysburg
Gwynedd-Mercy College, Gwynedd Valley
Haverford College, Haverford
Holy Family College, Philadelphia
Immaculata College, Immaculata
Indiana University of Pennsylvania, Indiana
King's College, Wilkes-Barre
Lafayette College, Easton
La Salle College, Philadelphia
Lebanon Valley College, Annville
Lehigh University, Bethlehem
Lincoln University, Lincoln University
Lock Haven State College, Lock Haven
Lycoming College, Williamsport
Mansfield State College, Mansfield
Marywood College, Scranton
Mercyhurst College, Erie
Messiah College, Grantham
Millersville State College, Millersville
Moravian College, Bethlehem
Mount Mercy College, Pittsburgh
Muhlenberg College, Allentown
Saint Charles Seminary, Philadelphia
Saint Fidelis College, Herman
Saint Francis College, Loretto
Saint Joseph's College, Philadelphia
Saint Vincent College, Latrobe

Seton Hill College, Greensburg
Shippensburg State College, Shippensburg
Susquehanna University, Selinsgrove
Temple University, Philadelphia
University of Pennsylvania, Philadelphia
University of Pittsburgh, Pittsburgh
University of Scranton, Scranton
Ursinus College, Collegeville
Villa Maria College, Erie
Villanova University, Villanova
Washington and Jefferson College, Washington
Waynesburg College, Waynesburg
West Chester State College, West Chester
Westminster College, New Wilmington
Wilkes College, Wilkes-Barre
Wilson College, Chambersburg

PUERTO RICO

College of the Sacred Heart, Santurce
University of Puerto Rico, Mayagüez Campus, Mayagüez

RHODE ISLAND

Barrington College, Barrington
Brown University, Providence
University of Rhode Island, Kingston

SOUTH CAROLINA

Allen University, Columbia
Benedict College, Columbia
The Citadel, Charlestown
Columbia Bible College, Columbia
Columbia College, Columbia
Erskine College, Due West
Morris College, Sumter
Newberry College, Newberry
South Carolina State College, Orangeburg
University of South Carolina, Columbia
Wofford College, Spartanburg

SOUTH DAKOTA

Black Hills State College, Spearfish
Dakota Wesleyan University, Mitchell
Huron College, Huron
Mount Marty College, Yankton
Northern State College, Aberdeen
Sioux Falls College, Sioux Falls
South Dakota State University, Brookings
Southern State College, Springfield
University of South Dakota, Vermillion
Yankton College, Yankton

TENNESSEE

Austin Peay State College, Clarksville
Belmont College, Nashville
Bethel College, McKenzie
Carson-Newman College, Jefferson City
Christian Brothers College, Memphis
Covenant College, Lookout Mountain
David Lipscomb College, Nashville
East Tennessee State University, Johnson City
George Peabody College for Teachers, Nashville
King College, Bristol
Knoxville College, Knoxville
LeMoyne College, Memphis
Lincoln Memorial University, Harrogate
Maryville College, Maryville
Memphis State University, Memphis
Middle Tennessee State University, Murfreesboro
Milligan College, Milligan College
Siena College, Memphis
Southern Missionary College, Collegedale
Southwestern at Memphis, Memphis
Tennessee Temple College, Chattanooga
Tennessee Wesleyan College, Athens
Tusculum College, Greeneville
Union University, Jackson
University of the South, Sewanee
University of Tennessee, Knoxville
Vanderbilt University, Nashville

TEXAS

Abilene Christian College, Abilene
Austin College, Sherman
East Texas Baptist College, Marshall
East Texas State University, Commerce
Hardin-Simmons University, Abilene
Howard Wayne College, Brownwood
Huston-Tillotson College, Austin
Incarnate Word College, San Antonio
Jarvis Christian College, Hawkins
LeTourneau College, Longview
Mary Hardin–Baylor College, Belton
McMurry College, Abilene
Midwestern University, Wichita Falls
Rice University, Houston
St. Edward's University/Maryhill College, Austin
St. Mary's University, San Antonio
Southwest Texas State College, San Marcos
Southwestern University, Georgetown
Stephen F. Austin State College, Nacogdoches

Sul Ross State College, Alpine
Tarleton State College, Stephenville
Tennessee Wesleyan College, Athens
Texas A&M University, College Station
Texas Christian University, Fort Worth
Texas College of Arts and Industries, Kingsville
Texas Lutheran College, Seguin
Texas Southern University, Houston
Texas Technological College, Lubbock
Texas Women's University, Denton
University of Corpus Christi, Corpus Christi
University of Dallas, University of Dallas Station
University of St. Thomas, Houston
University of Texas, Austin
University of Texas: Arlington State College, Arlington
University of Texas at El Paso–Texas Western College, El Paso
West Texas State University, Canyon

UTAH

College of Southern Utah, Cedar City
University of Utah, Salt Lake City
Utah State University, Logan
Westminster College, Salt Lake City

VERMONT

Goddard College, Plainfield
Marlboro College, Marlboro
Middlebury College, Middlebury
Norwich University, Northfield
St. Michael's College, Winooski
University of Vermont, Burlington
Windham College, Putney

VIRGINIA

Bridgewater College, Bridgewater
College of William and Mary, Williamsburg
Eastern Mennonite College, Harrisonburg
Frederick College, Portsmouth
Hampden-Sydney College, Hampden-Sydney
Hampton Institute, Hampton
Hollins College, Hollins College
Longwood College, Farmville
Madison College, Harrisonburg
Mary Baldwin College, Staunton
Mary Washington College of the University of Virginia, Fredericksburg
Radford College, Radford
Randolph-Macon College, Ashland
Roanoke College, Salem
Sweet Briar College, Sweet Briar

University of Richmond, Richmond
University of Richmond, Westhampton College, Richmond
University of Virginia, Charlottesville
Virginia Military Institute, Lexington
Virginia Polytechnic Institute, Blacksburg
Virginia State College, Petersburg
Virginia Union University, Richmond
Washington and Lee University, Lexington

WASHINGTON

Central Washington State College, Ellensburg
Eastern Washington State College, Cheney
Gonzaga University, Spokane
St. Martin's College, Olympia
Seattle Pacific College, Seattle
Seattle University, Seattle
University of Washington, Seattle
Walla Walla College, College Place
Western Washington State College, Bellingham
Whitman College, Walla Walla
Whitworth College, Spokane

WEST VIRGINIA

Alderson-Broaddus College, Philippi
Bethany College, Bethany
Concord College, Athens
Davis and Elkins College, Elkins
Fairmont State College, Fairmont
Glenville State College, Glenville
Morris Harvey College, Charleston
Salem College, Salem
Shepherd College, Shepherdstown
West Liberty State College, West Liberty
West Virginia State College, Institute
West Virginia University, Morgantown
West Virginia Wesleyan College, Buckhannon
Wheeling College, Wheeling

WISCONSIN

Alverno College, Milwaukee
Beloit College, Beloit
Carroll College, Waukesha
Carthage College, Kenosha
Dominican College, Racine
Edgewood College, Madison
Holy Family College, Manitowoc
Lakeland College, Sheboygan
Lawrence University, Appleton
Marian College of Fond du Lac, Fond du Lac

Milton College, Milton
Mount Mary College, Milwaukee
Mount St. Paul College, Waukesha
Mount Senario College, Ladysmith
Northland College, Ashland
Ripon College, Ripon
St. Francis College, Burlington
St. Francis Seminary, Milwaukee
St. Norbert College, West De Pere
Stout State University, Menomonie
University of Wisconsin, Madison
Wisconsin State University, Eau Claire
Wisconsin State University, La Crosse
Wsconsin State University, River Falls
Wisconsin State University, Stevens Point
Wisconsin State University, Superior
Wisconsin Sttae University, Whitewater

WYOMING

University of Wyoming, Laramie